P9-CKX-137

JUN 2 7 2024

DAVID O. McKAY LIBRARY
BYU-IDAHO

JUN 9 7 2024

*The
Two Lives of
Joseph Conrad*

The
Two Lives of
Joseph Conrad

BY LEO GURKO

Thomas Y. Crowell Company

New York

Acknowledgment is made to the following publishers for granting permission to quote from copyrighted works:

J. M. Dent & Sons Ltd. and the Trustees of the Joseph Conrad Estate, for quotations from Conrad's letters and from *The Collected Edition of the Works of Joseph Conrad*.

The Bobbs-Merrill Company for the selections from *Letters from Joseph Conrad, 1895–1924,* edited with an introduction by Edward Garnett, copyright 1928 by The Bobbs-Merrill Company, Inc., copyright © 1956 by David Garnett.

Charles Scribner's Sons for the passages from *Castles in Spain,* by John Galsworthy, and *The Life and Letters of John Galsworthy,* by H. V. Marrot.

Yale University Press for the quotations from *Letters of Joseph Conrad to Marguerite Poradowska, 1890–1920,* translated and edited by John A. Gee and Paul J. Sturm.

New York University Press for the selections from *Stephen Crane: Letters,* edited by R. W. Stallman and Lillian Gilkes.

Copyright © 1965 by Leo Gurko

ALL RIGHTS RESERVED. NO PART OF THIS BOOK MAY
BE REPRODUCED IN ANY FORM, EXCEPT BY A REVIEWER,
WITHOUT THE PERMISSION OF THE PUBLISHER.

DESIGNED BY WLADISLAW FINNE

MANUFACTURED IN THE UNITED STATES OF AMERICA
BY THE VAIL-BALLOU PRESS, INC., BINGHAMTON, NEW YORK

LIBRARY OF CONGRESS CATALOG CARD NO. 65-16180

FIRST PRINTING

Again for Miriam

FEB 7 '80

By the Author

THE ANGRY DECADE

HEROES, HIGHBROWS AND THE POPULAR MIND

TOM PAINE, FREEDOM'S APOSTLE

JOSEPH CONRAD: GIANT IN EXILE

THE TWO LIVES OF JOSEPH CONRAD

FOREWORD

DEC. 3 1857

There are three remarkable things about Joseph Conrad. First, he led two lives: twenty years as a seaman, mate, and captain, followed by thirty as a writer. In this double existence on both sea and land, he enjoyed adventures and overcame obstacles that would have stopped an ordinary man.

Second, as a writer he became one of the great modern artists. His novels and short stories are among the masterpieces of our literature.

Third, he wrote in a language twice removed from his own. Polish was his native tongue; French, the language he acquired next. By his twentieth year he still did not know a word of English. Yet he became one of the masters of English prose. And not just of a common, garden variety, but of a prose peculiarly rich and powerful. It was said by one of his friends that Conrad did not learn English, he seized it by the throat and conquered it.

Conrad wrote nearly four thousand letters, and these are a principal source of information about his life. Not all of them were preserved, nor have they all been published. The most important, however, have already appeared in print. A large number were included in G. Jean-Aubry's two-volume *Joseph Conrad, Life and Letters.* Those to Edward Garnett, the literary critic who became Conrad's friend, to Marguerite Poradowska, Conrad's cousin by marriage, to Richard Curle, a young friend of his last years, and to William Blackwood, who published several of Conrad's stories in *Blackwood's Magazine,* came out in separate volumes. A collection of Conrad's letters to and from his Polish friends has also appeared.

Mrs. Conrad wrote two books of reminiscences about her husband. Richard Curle and Ford Madox Ford, a friend and collaborator of Conrad in his early period, published personal memoirs about him. There have been two significant biographies: the book by Jean-Aubry already mentioned and a more detailed and recent study by Jocelyn Baines. Various letters and documents written by Conrad's relatives in Poland, and now in the national libraries at Warsaw and Cracow, are other valuable sources.

The most comprehensive group of Conrad manuscripts and material in the world is the George T. Keating collection at Yale University. Important, though less extensive, is the Conrad material in the Berg Room of the New York Public Library and in the Rosenbach collection in Philadelphia. Letters, documents, and records of many kinds are in the possession of the Morgan library, the Harvard University library, the British Museum, and various individual collectors.

I am grateful to J. M. Dent & Sons Ltd. and the Trustees of the Joseph Conrad Estate for permission to quote from Conrad's letters and works, and to The Macmillan Company, which published an earlier book of mine, *Joseph Conrad: Giant in Exile,* from which I have drawn a number of ideas.

CONTENTS

The
Two Lives of
Joseph Conrad

CHAPTER 1

The Plight of Poland

On a cold winter day in 1863, prisoner No. 23 wandered about in the snow of the Vologda prison camp in northern Russia. He was the smallest and youngest inmate, a boy of five, sharing his father's exile in this frozen waste. There were no other children his own age, no schools, no playgrounds, no comforts, and only the two Vologda seasons: the "green" winter and the "white" winter.

The boy's name was Józef Teodor Konrad Nalecz Korzeniowski. The world would some day know him as Joseph Conrad.

He was born on December 3, 1857, near Berdichev, a small town in the Polish Ukraine. His family called him by the third of his names, Konrad. This was in honor of Konrad Wallenrod, the hero of the epic

1

by Adam Mickiewicz, Poland's great national poet.

The Korzeniowskis were fire-eating patriots: Apollo Korzeniowski, Conrad's father, was to be arrested by the Russian police for conspiring to free Poland from the hated rule of the czar. He would be exiled to a remote corner of Russia and eventually die for the cause of Polish independence. One of Conrad's great-uncles had fought in the army of Napoleon which, at the beginning of the century, had freed Poland from another Russian czar.

The modern history of Poland has been tragically unhappy. A cruel geography surrounded her with three powerful and aggressive states: Russia, Prussia, and the Austro-Hungarian Empire. Late in the eighteenth century they invaded Poland and partitioned her. The largest section, and eventually the capital city of Warsaw, went to Russia; the second, in the northwest, to Prussia; and the third, in the southwest, to Austro-Hungary.

The Poles did not take this division meekly. An ardently independent and patriotic people, they revolted against their oppressors at regular intervals and clung jealously to their national identity, which no amount of Russian or Prussian force was able to suppress. France was Poland's traditional ally. Napoleon, who had conquered so many peoples, was, ironically, the liberator of the Poles. But with the downfall of Napoleon, Poland once again fell into the hands of her greedy neighbors. This latest occupation had already lasted more than forty years when Conrad was born.

Like all Poles of his century, he grew up in a feverish atmosphere of conspiracy and rebellion. His country was painfully divided between its dream of independence and the reality of occupation. This theme of the divided self, of the man pulled one way by an ideal and another by actuality, was to recur again and again in the novels he would one day write, a theme impressed upon him during his tenderest years by the plight of Poland.

His family was also divided, between his father's side and his mother's. The Korzeniowskis had always been hotheads, eager to rise up against the Russian oppressor whether the moment was opportune or not. They scorned caution, squandered the family estates through rash speculation and bad management, and would gladly have given up the prospect of reasonable success tomorrow for the sake of immediate action today. The Bobrowskis, his mother's people, were equally patriotic but considerably more prudent and far more skeptical of the prospects for Polish freedom. They were willing to bide their time, meanwhile living as best they could under the oppressor. They looked upon the Korzeniowskis with intense distrust and suspicion. When Apollo came courting Evelina Bobrowska, Conrad's mother, her father refused to allow the marriage. It did not take place until after the father's death eight years later.

By that time the Korzeniowski property had been lost, and Apollo was forced to manage the estates of others. The newly married couple moved to the south of Poland, where Conrad was born. Apollo, however, did not prosper in his new occupation, and began looking about for something else to do. His real love had always been literature. He had written verse plays, and translated Shakespeare, Dickens, Hugo, and other writers into Polish. When Conrad was three, his father went to Warsaw, hoping to pursue a literary career.

In normal times he might have become a professional man of letters as a matter of course. But the times were abnormal, and once he reached the capital he was quickly swept up in the nationalist movement. This aggravated the moody, restless strain in his temperament. He joined the Polish underground, which was plotting an uprising against the czar. He had as little talent for conspiratorial politics as for estate management, and in 1861 was arrested by the czarist police.

The Russians regarded him as a dangerous man. He was an intellectual or, in the epithet common in Eastern Europe, a member of the intelligentsia. In a country where most of the people were illiterate peasants, the role played by educated men was crucially important. They were the natural leaders of their country. Where they led, the masses followed. If they opposed the Russians, the Russians could count on the hostility of the population as a whole. The elimination or neutralization of the educated Poles was therefore a key Russian policy.

Apollo Korzeniowski also belonged to the landowning class. Above him in the social scale was a small group of wealthy and powerful aristocrats, fiercely patriotic and fiercely anti-Russian. Below him was the large mass of peasants. Polish authority, in a country that was still semifeudal, came traditionally from the aristocracy and landed gentry. Thus, both his class connections and his activities as a writer made Apollo a threat to the Russian regime.

He was condemned to exile in Russia itself. His failure as a political figure is underlined by what followed. When the great Polish uprising of 1863 erupted, he was a helpless prisoner hundreds of miles away in northern Russia.

It was the surprising practice of the Russian government to allow the wives and children of political prisoners to accompany them. Permission was granted Evelina Korzeniowska and her small son to make the long journey with Apollo to the Vologda prison camp. There they were given registration numbers: the father was No. 21; the mother, No. 22; and Conrad, No. 23. Living conditions were bleak, the weather freezing. Evelina, none too robust physically, suffered under these hostile elements and, in 1865, died. Conrad, now seven, was thrown into the exclusive company of his father. They remained together another four years, until Apollo's death from tuberculosis in 1869.

These four years in Conrad's lonely boyhood were lightened by literature and books. His father was allowed to carry on his work as a translator, and he would often read aloud to the boy from his translations of French and English writers. Conrad himself occasionally stole into his father's study and read from the galley proofs.

Shakespeare seems to have made an especially deep impression upon him even at that early age. In Shakespeare there is the recurring theme of the miscast man forced into situations contrary to his nature. Hamlet is trapped in a time he finds "out of joint"; Othello is driven to kill the person he loves most dearly; the quiet, reflective Brutus is forced to become an assassin. Conrad's father was also forced to do things he was not fitted for, because of his birth in a country betrayed by geography and history. To young Conrad the plays of Shakespeare were demonstrations of the same pattern. They provided an imaginative version of what life was all about.

Conrad's childhood was spent under abnormal conditions. He lived in an enemy country, without companions of his own age. His parents died slowly before his eyes. The nervous impressionability that was to mark him as a man was ruthlessly stamped upon him as a boy. Long before he began to think for himself, he was influenced by the attitudes of his parents: his father's passionate rebelliousness, his mother's quiet acceptance and endurance.

Very little is known of Conrad's mother. But his father emerges clearly as a man torn between two powerful forces pulling him in opposite directions. His nature and native talents inclined him to an intellectual life. The circumstances and atmosphere of Poland drove him to the political action he was not equipped to handle. The times were as "out of joint" for him as for Hamlet. In a letter written more than thirty years later, Conrad recalled his father as:

> A man of great sensibilities; of exalted and dreamy temperament; with a terrible gift of irony and of gloomy disposition. His aspect was distinguished; his conversation very fascinating; but his face, in repose sombre, lighted all over when he smiled. I remember him well.

This tormented man is the one constant figure in his son's novels.

In the last months of his life, when the signs of approaching death were already visible upon him, Apollo was allowed to return to Poland. He chose to live—or rather, to die—in Cracow, Poland's second city. There he was hailed as a great patriot and showered with whatever honors his countrymen could bestow.

Cracow, in the Austrian zone, was an appropriate setting for the dying man. Its greatness as a city had come during the Middle Ages, when the kingdom of Poland was first founded. It was filled with many splendid churches, monuments, and mausoleums— souvenirs of its once glorious past. But the glory had long since ended, and Cracow was now feeding on ancient memories no longer connected with the drab present. It was a magnificently preserved cemetery, and here Apollo died, leaving behind him an only son, orphaned at eleven.

He was given a great public funeral, befitting a man

who had martyred himself, however ineffectually, for the national cause. Three years later Conrad received the freedom of the city as a last tribute to his father, now enshrined in the myth of Poland.

CHAPTER 2

A Strange Ambition

With both parents gone, Conrad was turned over to the care of his maternal uncle, Tadeusz Bobrowski, in Cracow. Uncle Tadeusz was a true Bobrowski. He believed in accepting the world as it was and making the most of it. He loved Poland and would have done much to set her free, but it is doubtful that he would have gone to extremes. If it came to a choice between living in chains and dying for freedom, he would certainly have chosen to live. The chains might one day be removed; but life, once gone, could never be restored.

He was a prudent realist who looked upon the career of his departed brother-in-law as childish heroics. Uncle Tadeusz believed in hard work, thrift, personal ambition—all the middle-class virtues which depend for their existence upon a stable social order. Better a stable order under the czar, for the time being at any rate, than hopeless turmoil in the hands of those naïve revolutionary nationalists whose idealism demanded total sacrifice without any reasonable hope of success.

Uncle Tadeusz was a great advocate of the possible, of the task at hand. In work, and particularly in work sanctioned by society, lay man's salvation. Society alone could foster the discretion and responsibility that the uncle hoped to encourage in the nephew whose guardian he had become. He was determined to subdue and control the impulsive Korzeniowski strain in Conrad.

It was a moody eleven-year-old whom Uncle Tadeusz had inherited and now had on his hands. Much of the time the boy was irritable and withdrawn. But now and then he would abruptly emerge from his self-imposed reserve and become spontaneous and even gay. One of his early companions, Jadwiga Kalucka, recalled him as a lively boy of unusual intelligence. He spent several holidays with her family in Lwow. He wrote skits, organized amateur theatricals, displayed high spirits, and generally charmed the household. At home, however, he tended to relapse into moody silences. The early shocks he had suffered had left their mark.

The traditional set of attitudes that most boys of that day almost automatically adopted did not seem to take hold of Conrad. He did not believe in the competence, let alone the superiority of his teachers; they frankly bored him. Although he was always on good terms with his relatives, they failed to inspire him with any highly developed family sense. He was born and brought up as a Roman Catholic, yet religion never stirred him deeply; he was to grow up a nonbeliever. As to Poland, though he was as patriotic as most Poles, he had no intention of following in his father's footsteps and joining the political underground.

Conrad spent five years as a schoolboy in Cracow. Like all educated Poles and Russians of the time, he was taught to speak French as a matter of course. Most of the other subjects left him cold. He found the academic routine dull, and the instructors far less exciting and cultivated than his father. He did like geography, but even geography was taught, he remembered later, by "mere bored professors who were not only middle-aged but looked to me as if they had never been young."

The geography that aroused him was not taught in the classroom. He came upon it through random reading in the books of explorers like Mungo Park and Captain Cook. Park had navigated the headwaters of the Niger, and Cook had explored the Pacific regions. These men made him aware of places far from home and freed his imagination from the enclosed life of Poland. One day he shut his eyes and poked his finger blindly into a map of the world. His finger touched central Africa. "I shall go there some day," he resolved.

A strange ambition took root in Conrad's mind. He began to dream of going off to sea. The more he thought about it the stronger it grew. In Poland at that time, this was a preposterous idea. No Pole within living memory had been a sailor. Poland was then a landlocked country, without a navy or merchant marine of its own. To go to sea meant leaving Poland altogether. This struck everyone as an act of political desertion. A great outcry arose in Conrad's little world, from his guardian, friends, relatives, the community in Cracow that revered the memory of his father.

At first, the thought of Conrad becoming a seaman was laughed off as boyish nonsense. When he persisted, a general family alarm was sounded and everyone, in his own way, tried to rid the youth of his absurd fancy. He was talked to, reasoned with, shouted at, lectured, scolded. There were family conferences in which the issue, now becoming critical, was anxiously discussed. The most telling argument raised against Conrad was the charge of treason. He was abandoning Poland in her hour of greatest need, when she required her young men most. This was an act of unspeakable selfishness; he would never be forgiven for it, either in his own conscience or in the hearts of his countrymen. To this accusation he had no answer. He said nothing, but clung the more stubbornly to his desire.

Uncle Tadeusz was the most persistent, persuasive, and in many ways the gentlest of his opponents. He tried everything within reason to wean Conrad away from his obsession. In the summer of 1873, when his nephew was fifteen, he engaged a medical student from the University of Cracow to accompany Conrad on a walking tour of Switzerland. The student's special assignment was to drive the mischievous notion out of Conrad's head. To no avail. Conrad enjoyed the tour and his tutor's company, but came home as firmly resolved as ever.

As a last resort, his guardian proposed that he apply for a commission in the Austrian navy. Austria was the least obnoxious of the partitioning powers, and the life of a naval officer, while in all truth strange enough for a Pole, was at least a respectable career for a gentleman. Conrad would have none of it. He wanted to get out of Poland and her unhappy situation altogether. The larger world, outside the closed societies of central Europe, drew him irresistibly.

The scandal and uproar, the pressure upon him to give up what was generally regarded as a lunatic notion were very great. In his autobiographical memoir *A Personal Record,* written thirty-five years later, Conrad recalled the shocked opposition as though it had happened the day before.

> I don't mean to say that a whole country had been convulsed by my desire to go to sea. But for a boy between fifteen and sixteen, sensitive enough, in all conscience, the commotion of his little world had seemed a very considerable thing indeed. So considerable that, absurdly enough, the echoes of it linger to this day. I catch myself in hours of solitude and retrospect meeting arguments and charges made thirty-five years ago by voices now forever still; finding things to say that

an assailed boy could not have found, simply because of the mysteriousness of his impulses to himself. I understood no more than the people who called upon me to explain myself. There was no precedent. I verily believe mine was the only case of a boy of my nationality and antecedents taking a, so to speak, standing jump out of his racial surroundings and associations.

Where indeed had these impulses come from? It was true that the explorers he read and loved had traveled over the sea. And he had also been fascinated by the sea novels of Hugo, Marryat, and Fenimore Cooper. But the answer lay in life rather than literature. The feeling had grown steadily in him that the Polish cause was hopeless, that national independence was only a dream, beautiful no doubt, but futile. His ancestors had died for Poland, gloriously perhaps, but vainly. He had seen the lives of his parents sacrificed to their unhappy country. No matter how much he loved Poland and prayed for her independence, he had no intention of throwing his own life away for her sake. To this extent, he had plainly absorbed the lessons of his guardian and was determined to avoid the fruitless sacrifices of his father.

The pressures exerted to keep him from taking the "jump out of his racial surroundings" aggravated an already high-strung temper. He gave way to ironic outbursts, much like his father's, followed by aloof silences when no one could reach him. The argument between himself and his relatives made him moodier than ever and harder to get along with. In the end, reluctantly and filled with doubts and misgivings, his uncle let him go.

But where to? He could not go anywhere, just at random. There was one logical destination, and really only one—France. It was the European country to which Poland felt closest. Napoleon, who was still worshipped in his own country, was worshipped in Poland also, as a liberator. The rest of Europe may have rejoiced in Waterloo as the defeat of a tyrant, but Poland, like France, mourned it as a calamity. French newspapers, books, and ideas circulated freely in Poland. All educated Poles spoke French as their second language, and French prestige in their eyes was enormous.

Moreover, France had a special advantage for a boy who wanted to be a sailor. She was a great seagoing power, with a navy, a merchant fleet, and numerous ports not only in Europe but in her colonial territories which stretched around the world. France had maritime traditions and maritime connections, all of which would encourage, nurture, and reward a career at sea.

Uncle Tadeusz agreed to send Conrad to France. It was typical of the man that once he decided to accept the new state of affairs he did so with good grace and great common sense. He arranged a monthly allowance for Conrad from the legacy left by Apollo and gave him letters of introduction to French acquaintances.

On October 26, 1874, Conrad boarded the express for Marseilles. "I got into the train as a man gets into a dream," was the way he remembered it long afterward. He was still six weeks short of his seventeenth birthday, but in some ways he was mature beyond his years. The harshness of his early life had darkened his youthful spirit, but had not destroyed it. It had strengthened the vein of melancholy in him, the melancholy that in later years was to break out into periods of lingering depression.

Conrad carried with him on the train to France an odd assortment of attitudes and accomplishments: a highly developed sense of tragedy, an appetite for adventure and excitement, the polished manners that were traditional with the Polish gentry, and a facility in two languages, Polish and French. The knowledge of French would be put to use at once. It was the key to Conrad's second country.

CHAPTER 3

France

Most Polish travelers and émigrés headed for Paris, and relatives of the Bobrowskis had settled there. Conrad, however, went straight to Marseilles.

There was a compelling reason for this. Marseilles was the greatest seaport on the Mediterranean, and the logical starting place for a boy who wanted to go to sea. It was the exit point from France to the rest of the world, and it was the rest of the world that Conrad had a vague yet powerful urge to explore.

There were two societies in Marseilles, sharply divided from one another. There was the society of the waterfront: sailors, pilots, adventurers, and riffraff from every continent, men dodging the police, men on the make, deadbeats of every conceivable kind, a lively world of rough, unsettled, rootless human beings. There, things were never the same from one day to another. Like the water itself, life was in constant flux.

To a young foreigner hungry for new impressions, this dramatic scene was a powerful magnet. Conrad hung about the waterfront, made friends with harbor pilots, and was often taken along on the pilot boats which went out to the ships entering and leaving the harbor. A landmark which he passed on these occasions was the Château d'If, the grim island dungeon where, in Dumas' novel, the Count of Monte Cristo had been imprisoned. Conrad became a favorite of the Marseilles pilots, their "Polish mascot," and was patronized by them with good-humored affection. He soon added a strong southern accent to the formal French he had learned at school.

At the other end of the scale, there was the established society of Marseilles. This consisted of the well-to-do families who had been settled in the town for generations; they lived in fine houses, cultivated the arts, held salons, and, while making their money from Marseilles' bustling trade with the outside world, in private life kept clear of the waterfront. Here were the merchants, bankers, shipowners—men whose opinions were fiercely conservative, who stood for stability and order, even the old reactionary order, as against change and reform.

Prominent among them were the Delestangs, to whom Conrad had a letter of introduction. M. Delestang owned a merchant fleet, and it was through him that Conrad got his first job at sea. The Delestang ships were in the West Indian trade, touching at Haiti, Martinique, Guadeloupe, and other Caribbean islands. Conrad signed on as an able-bodied seaman aboard the Delestang vessel the *Saint-Antoine,* and in 1875 and 1876 made a number of voyages—his maiden voyages —to the Caribbean.

It was during these journeys that he met the man who was to exercise a major influence on his imagination during his French years. This was Dominic Cervoni, first mate of the *Saint-Antoine.* Cervoni was a Corsican, a ruggedly built, handsome, masterful figure, a born leader who could discipline the men under him yet win their wholehearted respect.

Cervoni took a liking to the Polish apprentice in his crew. With Conrad, it was a case of hero worship at first sight. The first mate seemed to him everything a man should be: skillful at his trade, self-possessed, faithful to the ideals of bravery and duty, and fascinating in conversation, a conversation spiced by the endless anecdotes of a richly varied life at sea. He became the model for Nostromo, the "magnificent capataz de cargadores," in the great novel bearing that name which Conrad was to write nearly thirty years later. They were an oddly assorted pair—the veteran mate who spoke French with an Italian accent and the greenest mariner aboard, twenty years his junior, who spoke French with a Polish accent. In their relationship, there was a touch of teacher and pupil and of father and son.

In the spring of 1876 Cervoni and Conrad went off together on a private venture of their own. The *Saint-Antoine* was in Haiti, where it was scheduled to remain for a few weeks while the owners negotiated for cargo before the trip home. Rather than hang around the port doing nothing, the two men hired themselves out on a schooner running a clandestine shipment of arms to a Central American republic involved in civil war. The vessel made its way across the Gulf of Mexico, delivered its arms successfully, returned for another load, and repeated the process.

The Corsican and the Pole, temporarily on leave from their French ship, smuggled guns up and down the coast of Central America. There was no shortage of markets. Wars and revolutions were a chronic part of the landscape. Some weeks later they got as far south as Venezuela, where Conrad landed and spent a few hours. From here they made their way back to the *Saint-Antoine*.

This adventurous little episode was a prelude to a much more dangerous adventure in gunrunning that the two friends became involved in after their return to Marseilles. Conrad was drawn into it by his contact with the Delestangs.

The Delestangs were fanatical monarchists who prayed and worked for a return of the king. In 1870 France had suffered a crushing defeat in the Franco-Prussian War. The emperor, Louis Napoleon, was overthrown and the Third Republic established. By 1875 France had recovered from the war and was enjoying an economic boom under the republican government. But the two great royalist factions, Bourbons and Bonapartists, were still numerous and hopeful of returning to power.

In that day such hopes did not seem unreal or far-fetched. Only a few years had passed since a Bonaparte had ruled France. He had held power for more than twenty years and had been unseated, not by internal discontent, but by a German invasion. For thirty years before this, Bourbon kings had occupied the throne. There were royalist groups all over France, led by ambitious men who fervently believed that the monarchy or empire would soon be restored.

The French royalists worked for monarchy even in other countries. The favorite foreign cause of the Delestangs, and their circle of friends and sympathizers in the south of France, was that of Don Carlos of Spain. His claim to the Spanish throne went back to 1833 when, upon the death of King Ferdinand VII, the crown passed to Ferdinand's daughter Isabel and not —as the Carlists insisted it should have by right of Salic law—to his younger brother Carlos. The Carlists fought two wars in the nineteenth century to regain the throne. The first was led by the original Don Carlos; the second by his son, the Don Carlos supported by the Delestangs. The Carlist stronghold was Navarre, in northern Spain; their insignia, the colorful red beret worn by their soldiers and partisans. For some years in the 1870s, they waged war against the government forces along a ragged front in the Basque country just south of the Pyrenees.

The Delestangs raised money and supplies for this war, recruited volunteers for the Carlist army, and propagandized tirelessly for the cause. Conrad was a natural prospect for them. He was young; he was a gentleman; he was obviously looking for action and excitement; and he was in debt to M. Delestang for having given him his start as a seaman. He joined up —not as a soldier in the trenches but as a smuggler of supplies to the Carlist army in the field, an operation in which he was already experienced.

More persuasive, perhaps, than the Delestangs in enlisting his aid for the Carlists was a young woman with whom he fell in love. Long afterward, in a semi-autobiographical novel *The Arrow of Gold,* dealing with his life in France, Conrad referred to her as Doña Rita. She was slightly older than Conrad, knew Don Carlos himself, and was an ardent Carlist follower. Rita returned Conrad's affection, though just what happened between her and Conrad is a mystery. In the warmth and ardor of this new emotional tie, Conrad flung himself into the Carlist cause with an enthusiasm that could not have been greater if he had really believed in it himself.

Conrad did not believe for a single moment in Carlism as a serious political movement. It was too plainly a lost cause. Nor was it devoted to some noble purpose: it did not seek to overthrow a foreign domination or a domestic tyranny. It simply wanted to substitute one king for another. And the present Don Carlos was a singularly graceless, mediocre, and ineffectual man. Even the Delestangs did not love or admire him. It was the royalist idea he embodied that bound them to him.

There was nothing in all this that moved Conrad one way or another. As a Pole he was, if anything, bored by lost causes. But as a youth he was responsive to the prospect of action, and if his sweetheart, friends, and employer were hotly in favor of anything, he needed no great urging to be in favor of it too.

Conrad and three of his friends scraped together all the money they could raise and bought a swift little sailing barque named the *Tremolino*. With Cervoni installed as skipper and his nephew César as one of the hands, they began ferrying guns and supplies to units of the Carlist army in northern Spain. Their two hazards were rough seas and the coastal surveillance of the Spanish navy. They managed to survive the first and for a time the second. Though sighted several times by government vessels, the *Tremolino,* fleet and maneuverable, had no great trouble escaping her pursuers. She might have done so to the end of the Carlist war and brought her owners handsome profits had she not been betrayed by a member of her own crew.

The villain was César. Out of greed and hatred for his uncle, who had kept him under strict discipline for years, he informed the Spanish police of the *Tremolino*'s course. During a landing operation she was trapped by a cutter which had been lying in ambush and now sealed off her escape. On the verge of capture Cervoni, with Conrad's permission, steered her onto the rocks. The barque splintered and sank. As she did, Cervoni, mortified by his nephew's treachery, felled him with a blow of his fist. César apparently sank to the bottom of the Mediterranean aboard the vessel he had betrayed, carrying with him the money he had been paid by the enemy. Actually, he survived the sinking of the *Tremolino* and lived to a ripe old age, always careful to stay out of his uncle's way. But Cervoni thought him dead and was thus appeased.

With his Corsican family pride restored, Cervoni helped Conrad and the others escape through enemy country. Luckily, the terrain of the Basque Pyrenees was rough, sparsely populated, and thinly patrolled. It was relatively easy to take cover when government troops appeared. Once they hid for hours in an underground cavern waiting for a group of soldiers, who had inconsiderately bivouacked nearby, to depart. The days were hot, the nights cold, the food only what they could find growing or get from friendly peasants. They were a battered, sorry-looking lot by the time they approached the Franco-Spanish border. The frontier, like the country through which they had passed, was loosely guarded. Smugglers and refugees had penetrated it easily in both directions for years. Conrad and his companions slipped past the Spanish guards at night and reached the safety of French soil. Relieved and exhausted, they made their way back to Marseilles.

Home again, free of the danger of capture and imprisonment, Conrad had time to take stock of his situation. In terms of money it was disastrous. The total loss of the *Tremolino* was a financial calamity. It had wiped away the savings he had managed to scrape together during his voyages to the West Indies. In addition, he had borrowed money from his uncle to invest in the Carlist enterprise, and this too was gone. He looked around desperately for some way of getting his money back in a hurry. There was really only one way—the gambling tables at Monte Carlo a short distance away. Conrad borrowed the little ready cash his friends had left, traveled to Monte Carlo in a mounting fever of anxiety and excitement, and tried his hand at roulette. He did not even have beginner's luck. After a few hours of hectic play, everything was lost. He returned to Marseilles utterly crushed.

There was always Uncle Tadeusz to fall back on. Since leaving Poland, Conrad had asked his uncle for help on several occasions. The money had been sent, accompanied by little lectures on the subject of his extravagance and instability. He could not turn to Uncle Tadeusz again. Not only was there a limit to how much money he felt he could take, but he was ashamed to admit his failure. This would only confirm his relatives' gloomy predictions of what his future outside Poland would be.

But money was not his only problem. There was also love. As long as he had Rita, his debts could somehow be borne. Late in 1877, however, even this saving relationship came to an end. The second Carlist war was now over, with only last-ditch elements of resistance still carrying on in Spain. Don Carlos himself had left the field of operations and returned to his headquarters in Paris. With him went his staff, his servants, and his advisers. With him, too, went Rita, leaving behind her in Marseilles a desolated, heartbroken Conrad with nothing left, he felt, to redeem the burden of his misfortunes.

One day early in 1878, while attending the Kiev Fair, Uncle Tadeusz received a telegram from Marseilles dispatched by one of Conrad's friends. He opened it and was profoundly shocked by what he read. The telegram announced that Conrad had been wounded and urged that money be sent and that Bobrowski himself come to France as soon as possible. In a state of great agitation, he wound up his business in Kiev at once. Sick with fear that Conrad was dying, that in fact he might not see him alive again, Uncle Tadeusz rushed to catch the next express to Marseilles. He paused only long enough to send a note about what was happening to an old family friend in Warsaw. To his relatives in Cracow he said nothing about Conrad's plight.

The express made good time on its westward journey, but it seemed agonizingly slow to the distraught guardian. At the Marseilles station Uncle Tadeusz hurried into a hansom and set off for Conrad's lodgings, fearing the worst. But when he arrived he discovered, to his immense relief, that Conrad was not dead, nor was he going to die. He was, in fact, plainly recovering. In an unusual outbreak of deep emotion, his eyes overflowing with tears, Uncle Tadeusz threw his arms around his errant nephew and kissed him warmly.

Once he had assured himself that the worst was over, Uncle Tadeusz began finding out what had happened. What he learned upset him profoundly once again: Conrad had shot himself in an attempt at suicide. There were plenty of reasons: the loss of the *Tremolino,* his mounting debts and his disastrous gambling, the unhappy end of his love affair, the galling humiliation of having to admit that perhaps his family was right and he had made a ghastly mistake in abandoning Poland.

Uncle Tadeusz also learned of another circumstance which had no doubt added to his nephew's distress. Conrad would soon be ineligible for the French merchant marine. There was a French law prohibiting the employment of foreign men aged twenty-one and over who were subject to military conscription in their own countries. Conrad would come of age on December 3, 1878. All these factors had pressed upon him, and in a moment of particularly acute depression, he had tried to kill himself.

In later life Conrad was to hint at a different version of how he was wounded. He would bare his breast, point proudly to a scar alongside his heart, and talk about a duel he had fought over the affections of a young woman in his far-off days as a youth in France. This was the story he encouraged his friend and biographer, Jean-Aubry, to believe. It was also the version he fictionalized in *The Arrow of Gold.* In that novel the young hero fights and is seriously wounded in a duel with a jealous American rival because of Doña Rita.

Conrad may have been reshaping his earlier life in a form more flattering to himself. It was easier for him to remember the episode as a romantic duel than as the more painful reality of suicide. Dueling was very much in the gallant tradition of the Polish gentry, as it was of the German and French. To think of oneself as a dashing youth fighting on the field of honor in defense of a young lady can be peculiarly comforting in later years. Also, suicide was a mortal sin to Catholics, and to camouflage it in a more acceptable light may have eased any feelings of guilt.

Whatever Conrad's reasons for changing the story, suicide and its causes became a principal theme of his novels and was obviously a subject about which he thought very deeply. Six of his major characters were to kill themselves. Captain Whalley, in "The End of the Tether," drowns himself from a sense of lost honor. Martin Decoud, in *Nostromo,* shoots himself because, trapped in a terrible solitude, he loses the sense of his own individuality. At the end of *The Secret Agent,* Winnie Verloc leaps to her death from a Channel steamer after murdering her husband and being abandoned by the man she thought would save her. In "The Planter of Malata," the central figure swims out to his death at sea when he is rebuffed by the woman he loves. Jorgenson, the faithful retainer in *The Rescue,* deliberately jumps into the hold of an ammunition ship with a lighted cigar in his mouth to prevent the gunpowder from falling into the hands of the enemy. And in the last chapter of *Victory,* Axel Heyst, when he finally realizes his incapacity to love, sets fire to his house and perishes in it.

Conrad healed rapidly, and, as so often happens, the

resort to violence had blown away his mood of depression. Though his situation had not changed, he felt—however irrationally—considerably more cheerful about it. His uncle too, convinced that Conrad would live, returned to his normal self. Now that Conrad was out of danger, Uncle Tadeusz proceeded to lecture him severely for his rashness and folly, and was more than ever confirmed in his distrust of the unstable Korzeniowski blood.

With his customary practicality, Uncle Tadeusz sat down with his nephew to discuss the next step. Conrad no longer had a future in France, at least not as a seaman. For emotional reasons too, he was anxious to leave the country and make a fresh start somewhere else.

But where? This question, first raised when the boy announced his intention of leaving Poland, now came up a second time. And once again there was only a single logical answer.

CHAPTER 4

A Second Exile

Conrad had spent four action-crammed years in France. He had gone to sea, fallen in love, taken part in political intrigue, attempted suicide, and lived through dangerous adventures and close escapes. But now, almost twenty-one and soon no longer eligible to serve in the French merchant fleet, the future was suddenly empty. France was closed to him. Where should he go?

The answer came almost by itself. Besides France, the other great European sea power was Great Britain. Unlike France, Britain had no age restrictions on foreigners serving in her merchant marine. England, then, was obviously Conrad's next step. Uncle Tadeusz thoroughly approved of England, but he would have approved of Siam or Timbuktu had it provided a haven for his wayward nephew.

Conrad decided to leave Marseilles as soon as he was able. Uncle Tadeusz, at his bedside, assured him that he must. His career had received a severe setback; all the more reason to resume it as soon as possible. Conrad agreed. France had lost all its attractions for him: the *Tremolino,* and with it all his money, lay at the bottom of the sea; Rita was gone; and the French marine service had no further use for him. It was time to move on.

He joined the crew of the first British freighter that came along. It was the *Mavis,* bound for the eastern Mediterranean. When he boarded the vessel, he could not speak a word of English. In fact, the only English he had even been aware of hearing till then was the cry "Look out there!" shouted to him by a sailor while Conrad was helping a Marseilles pilot transfer to a British ship. The three words meant nothing to him at the time, but he was to recall them later as his first introduction to the language which was to become "the speech of my secret choice, of my future, of long friendships, of the deepest affections . . . of thoughts pursued, of remembered emotions—of my very dreams!"

But that was later. At twenty, English was still so much gibberish to him. He had read some of the great English writers, like Shakespeare and Dickens, but only in Polish translations. He was coming to his new country like any other raw and unprepared foreigner.

Conrad was by no means the only non-Englishman on the *Mavis;* his ignorance of the language proved no great handicap. Sailing ships in the nineteenth century attracted crews from all nations, and apprentice mariners soon picked up the common argot of the sea. A kind of *lingua franca* was spoken in the forecastle. Captains and mates often barked orders at the crew in a gabble of words from French, Italian, Portuguese, and English that, on the merchant-marine level, were understood by everyone. The sea broke down ordinary frontiers and created its own community.

When Conrad came to write his first great sea tale, *The Nigger of the 'Narcissus,'* he created just such a community. The eighteen crewmen include a Finn, two Norwegians, and a West Indian Negro. The *Narcissus* is of British registry and its three officers are Englishmen. Yet they have no trouble telling the foreign hands what to do. In the novel, during the great storm that assails the ship on its run from Bombay to London, the crew performs valiantly under conditions of great stress without any breakdown in communication.

The *Mavis,* with Konrad Korzeniowski swabbing decks and standing watch, reached its destination in Constantinople, unloaded its cargo of coal, went on to the Sea of Azov where it took on a shipment of linseed, then headed back for England. The journey went off without incident, and in due course the *Mavis* landed at its home port of Lowestoft, a lively but rather dilapidated town on the Norfolk coast. Conrad left the ship and stood, for the first time, on British soil. It was June 18, 1878.

His arrival in England was very different from his experience in France. He had come to France with letters of introduction and with a thorough knowledge of the language and culture. In England he was a complete foreigner, unable to speak the language, and with no connections or introductions of any kind. For the first time since leaving Poland, he was overwhelmed by a sense of really being away from home, of being alone, in exile. He described these sensations later in his story "Amy Foster," in which Yanko Goorall, a Central European refugee, finds himself wretchedly alone on the alien English shore.

Conrad had to start from scratch and make a place for himself entirely on his own. First he had to find shelter in a strange port and establish a way of living. Then he had to look for another berth. For the first task he needed only a little money and some ingenuity. But the job of finding another vessel to ship out on was not so easy. Shipping was a notoriously unstable industry. It was nervously sensitive to the movements of business, the first to suffer in hard times, and almost the last to get back to normal during periods of recovery. It was an intensely competitive trade; shipowners had to bid for cargoes not only against their own countrymen but against those of other nations as well. A shipowner could never tell just when the next sailing would take place. Crews were not kept on permanently but assembled for only one voyage at a time.

A seaman's life was, therefore, transient and uncertain. After each voyage he was automatically unemployed and had to start all over again with each new ship. Between trips he earned nothing and had to spend his time presenting himself at the offices of ship-owners or hanging around the rough-and-ready employment agencies of the waterfront. Low pay, economic uncertainty, poor living conditions aboard ship combined to make a career at sea altogether risky and unstable, and led to a high rate of desertion among seamen.

Conrad was further handicapped by being a foreigner. There was no legal bar to his working on British ships, but in the nature of things native English sailors were given preference. As against outsiders they were the first to be signed on and, in slack times, the only ones. And Conrad could not conceal his foreignness. Long after he mastered English, he spoke it with a heavy accent.

Upon leaving the *Mavis*, Conrad was in no mood to grapple with his new situation. He squandered his wages on a spree, then wrote to his uncle asking for more money until he could find a new berth. He got a stinging letter in reply. His uncle denounced him for his extravagance: "I will not allow you to idle away your time at my cost; you will find help in me, but not for a lazybones and spendthrift. I have no money for drones and have no intention of working so that someone else may enjoy himself at my expense." He added a piece of advice: "Arrange your budget within the limits of what I give you, for I will give no more. Make no debts for I won't pay them. Commit no stupidities, for

I have no intention of making them good any more."
The letter, dated July 8, 1878, was accompanied by a
money order for six hundred francs, and a final word:
"You have forfeited my confidence. Work now to regain it."

Conrad, chastened for the moment, signed on with
The Skimmer of the Seas. This was the picturesque
name of an ordinary trading schooner plying the Norfolk coast. For three months he sailed between Lowestoft to the south and Newcastle to the north. The work
was dull and the landscape monotonous, but these
mattered little to Conrad. He enjoyed the rich Norfolk
dialect to which he was exposed and the new countryside he saw, even though it was the same strip of North
Sea coastline that kept passing before his eyes. He
called it "the school-room of my trade." There he
learned his first real English. His teachers were "the
sailors of the Norfolk shore; coast men, with steady
eyes, mighty limbs, and gentle voice; men of very few
words, which at least were never bare of meaning."

Conrad was as yet too young to mind the hard work
or the grubby conditions. After a while, however, he
began to long for the open sea and a chance to break
out of the confining coastal trade. In September a
newspaper advertisement inserted by a London shipping agent caught his eye. In response to it, he took a
train to the great capital and stepped into it "with
something of the feeling of a traveller penetrating into
a vast and unexplored wilderness." Wandering through
the crowded streets, he was filled with his usual mix-

ture of feelings: excitement at this tremendous pool of human energy, a certain depression at the vastness of London, at its anonymous multitude of faces, and a sense of emptiness which may have been present in the city or have been only a reflection of the fact that he knew no one in it. "No explorer could have been more lonely," he wrote in *Notes on Life and Letters* many years later. "I did not know a single soul of all these millions that all around me peopled the mysterious distances of the streets."

The image of himself as the eternal stranger in a strange country, an exciting, even wonderful country, yet one remaining wholly foreign to him, was already forming in his mind. He was the outside man perpetually doomed by circumstances to be looking in. This quickened his senses, sharpened his perceptions, made him more wary and alert. But it deprived him of a sense of belonging and the feeling of warmth that came with it.

His immediate mission in London was successful. He signed aboard the *Duke of Sutherland,* a wool clipper, and a month later, in October, 1878, set out for Australia. It was the first of a long series of voyages to the Pacific.

CHAPTER 5

Rise from the Fo'c'sle

The *Duke of Sutherland* reached Sydney in January, 1879, and Conrad did not return to England until October, a year after embarking. The long hours and exhausting labor before the mast, week after week on the endless sea, had worn him out and weakened his intention of remaining an ordinary seaman. One night in the Sydney dock, while he was standing watch, a man came aboard demanding refuge from the police. Conrad refused. The man abruptly drove a fist into his face, knocking him down. For days he sported a monumental shiner, which did not improve his spirits.

Back in England late in 1879, now approaching his twenty-second birthday, Conrad again found himself in a state of acute uncertainty. The year aboard the *Sutherland* had not been happy. He was homesick and wanted to return to Poland for a visit. His uncle, however, warned him against this. As a Pole, Conrad was technically a Russian citizen, liable for military service in the Russian army if he went home. Uncle Tadeusz urged Conrad to become a citizen of some other country. Almost any other would do. Since Conrad was now in the British merchant marine, English citizenship would be logical. But Swiss would do as well. Or Conrad could become a Yankee or a Laplander if he wished. Anything to escape the hated power of the Russians.

In an effort to improve his status and get a better job, Conrad asked his uncle to obtain from M. Delestang a letter of recommendation detailing his service on French ships. He was also seized with a longing to return to the Mediterranean, and in December, without waiting for the letter from M. Delestang, joined the *Europa,* a British vessel headed for Naples, Genoa, and Patras.

The journey on the *Europa* was thoroughly disagreeable. Conrad complained about the behavior of the captain, whom he thought mad, and again suffered from the hard work. Conrad was a rather small man, without, he was beginning to realize, the robust physique required of a professional seaman. It was one thing to spend a few strenuous years in his youth, sailing for the adventure of it, but a lifetime at sea was quite another matter. Climbing masts, handling heavy spars and ropes, wrestling with sail, often in high wind or storm, became a constant strain. Though steamships were replacing the old sailing vessels, most of Conrad's voyages were under sail. He infinitely preferred sail to steam. Sailing vessels gave him a much greater sense of personal participation in the running of the ship than did the more mechanized steamboats. But the physical labor required was far more grueling.

Conrad returned to London at the end of January, 1880, suffering from a heavy cold and an intermittent fever. He was again depressed and short of money. He had poured out his troubles to his uncle in a letter from Greece, and in February received a long reply. Uncle Tadeusz dismissed the complaints about the hard conditions of life at sea. These were to be expected. He chose to worry instead about his nephew's health, advised him to see a doctor, and cautioned him about the foggy London air.

Conrad thought seriously of leaving the sea altogether and accepting a post as secretary to a Canadian businessman. His uncle, however, scolded him severely for this. "I should not be your uncle or the man I am," he wrote, "if I did not say straight out that it is hopeless to throw yourself from one profession to another. Changes of that kind make men into those kinds of wasters who, as we say at home, have no friends and achieve nothing for themselves. You have chosen to be a sailor and I am sure that you will succeed without constantly changing your occupation."

Having bluntly expressed his own feelings in the matter, Uncle Tadeusz then turned around and disclaimed any intention of telling his nephew what to do. "That is my advice, but act in your own way, for in everything that concerns your career I leave you complete freedom, being ignorant of the circumstances in which you live. I have never been anything of an adventurer myself, and it is that fact which makes me wish regular employment for you."

These words reinforced an element in Conrad himself, the element of self-discipline and endurance, countering his restlessness and self-pity. He wanted to become a seaman worthy of the service, "good enough to work by the side of the men with whom I was to live." He was also driven by a necessity to succeed in a career disapproved of by everyone he knew. "I had to justify my existence to myself," he wrote, "to redeem a tacit moral pledge."

Very well, then, he would continue on the sea, but if the life of the ordinary sailor was too harsh for him, he would try to become an officer. He spent the spring of 1880 studying manuals of seamanship to prepare himself for a second mate's examination. There could be no more vivid evidence of his rapid progress in English than his ability to read and digest textbooks that were often highly technical. He took the examination at the beginning of June. After a three-hour ordeal with an elderly examiner who seemed to him unfriendly from the first, he was surprised and relieved to see the man push the coveted blue slip across the table to him. Overcome with joy, he found himself out on the street again, without being conscious of having gone down steps, "as if I had floated down the staircase."

He rushed to send the good news to Poland. The return letter from Uncle Tadeusz expressed a joy even greater than his own. "You have proved to your country and your family that you have not eaten unearned bread during these four years, that you have been able to overcome the drawbacks of being a foreigner without backing." The project of going to Canada was still pending, but the officer's ticket brought it to an end.

When Conrad informed his uncle of his decision to stick to the merchant marine, he received still another enthusiastic reply, dated June 28, 1880, in which Uncle Tadeusz reverted to his favorite theme of the Bobrowski–Nalecz Korzeniowski strains: "I see with pleasure that the 'Nalecz' in you has been modified by the influence of the Bobroszczaki, as your incomparable mother used to call her own family before she flew away to the nest of the 'Nalecz.' This time I rejoice over the influence of my family, though I don't deny the Naleczs a spirit of initiative and enterprise greater than that which runs in my veins. From the blend of these two famous races in your worthy person should spring a character so steadfast and energetic that the whole world will be astonished by it." This last prediction was to come true, though it was not as a sailor that Conrad would astonish the world.

Finding suitable berths as an officer was no easier than as an ordinary seaman. Almost three months passed before Conrad secured a post as third mate on the *Loch Etive,* a 1200-ton wool clipper bound for Sydney. Its skipper, Captain Stuart, had set records for

fast journeys on another vessel, the *Tweed*. He was irritated by the relative slowness of the *Loch Etive,* and
quarreled with the first mate incessantly all the way to
Australia and back. The second mate fell ill during the
journey, and Conrad was given special responsibilities,
which stimulated him and made his service aboard the
Loch Etive immensely different from anything he had
experienced in the fo'c'sle. He determined to qualify
for the next two examinations, first mate and captain,
as rapidly as possible.

The voyage lasted from August, 1880, to April,
1881. Then he again had trouble finding a berth, and
his chronic shortage of money returned to plague him.
He even told an outright lie to his uncle in order to ex-
tract ten pounds from him. In a letter asking for the
money, Conrad claimed to have shipped out on the
Annie Frost, which sank with all his worldly posses-
sions soon after leaving port. There was not a word of
truth in this. Conrad never signed on the *Annie Frost.*
His unsuspecting uncle sent him the ten pounds and remained ignorant of the fraud to the end of his days.

Oddly enough, Conrad was not depressed during
this period of unemployment or by the difficulties that
followed. His temperamental pattern had always been
one of sharp ups and downs, and he was now clearly in
an "up" phase. This was fortunate since his next voyage, as second mate aboard the ancient, leaky barque
Palestine, would have tried the patience of Job. Conrad, however, got through it almost cheerfully. The
vessel was very small, just 425 tons, and carried a crew
of only eight seamen and two cabin boys; its captain

and first mate were old men. Conrad was anxious to gain experience as second mate in order to qualify for his next examination, and was in no position to pick and choose.

The *Palestine* left London in September, 1881, for Newcastle, where she was to take on a shipment of coal for Bangkok. A tempest in the North Sea delayed her, and while waiting in the harbor at Newcastle, she was rammed by a steamer. It was not until late November that, with five hundred tons of coal aboard, she set out for Bangkok. But she got no farther than the English Channel when she was buffeted by gales and sprang a leak. She was forced to put in at Falmouth, the harbor in Cornwall, for repairs.

It was nine months before she sailed again, delayed by a whole series of nagging accidents. As the months dragged by, she became known far and wide as a jinxed ship. The harbor men laughed at her misfortunes and predicted that she would never sail again. Conrad spent part of his time reading Shakespeare, in English now, while repairmen hammered away at the ship in drydock. Once he collected three months' pay and went to London on a short leave. It took him only five days to spend the money—in music halls, bookstores, and expensive restaurants. He returned to Falmouth with a complete set of Byron's works, a new railway rug, and empty pockets.

At last, in September, 1882, the *Palestine* put to sea again. For a while all went smoothly. The barque crept down the African coast, passed through the Indian Ocean, then turned north toward Java. At noon on

March 11, 1883, smoke was discovered issuing from the hold. Water was poured on it and some tons of coal were thrown overboard, but three days later a mysterious explosion shook the old vessel. The second mate was thrown violently to the deck, and flames burned his hair, beard, and eyebrows. The fire spread, the *Palestine* was abandoned, and the crew took refuge in her three lifeboats.

One of them was commanded by Conrad—his first command. For hours he and the two crewmen accompanying him rowed and drifted in their open boat under a burning sun. At last, in the distance, they saw the high mountains of Sumatra. A puff of wind, "laden with the strange odours of blossoms, of aromatic wood," caressed their faces, "the first sigh of the East." This first glimpse of the Orient made an unforgettable impression on Conrad. "It was palpable and enslaving like a charm, like a whispered promise of mysterious delight."

They made their way slowly to shore in the gathering darkness, tied the boat to a wharf, and dropped into a heavy sleep. When they awoke, it was daylight, and there on the jetty, staring down at them in silence, were the men of the East. In the celebrated story "Youth," which Conrad later wrote about the *Palestine* experience, he described this climactic moment in a striking passage: "The whole length of the jetty was full of people. I saw brown, bronze, yellow faces, the black eyes, the glitter, the colour of an Eastern crowd. And all these beings . . . stared down at the sleeping men who at night had come to them from the sea.

Nothing moved. The fronds of palms stood still against the sky. Not a branch stirred along the shore, and the brown roofs of hidden houses peeped through the green foliage, through the big leaves that hung shining and still like leaves forged of heavy metal."

This spellbound moment invaded Conrad's imagination. He was to spend years among the Malays, but this first moment remained all-powerful. "For me all the East is contained in that vision of my youth. It is all in that moment when I opened my young eyes on it. I came upon it from a tussle with the sea—and I was young—and I saw it looking at me."

When the ship's company was reassembled, a British steamer took them to Singapore, where they arrived on March 22. A court of inquiry investigated the fate of the *Palestine* and acquitted the officers of any blame. Conrad stayed in Singapore through April, looking for an officer's berth back to England. No berth was forthcoming, and he was forced to return to Europe as a passenger on a steamship.

A year and a half of his life had been invested in the *Palestine*. He had nothing to show for it at the time except a few months of navigational experience. But he did get that first magical view of the exotic East. Later, the experience was to pay a handsome dividend by supplying the framework for "Youth."

Five years had passed since uncle and nephew had seen each other, and Uncle Tadeusz now arranged to have Conrad meet him in Marienbad, Germany, where he was taking the baths. Their reunion, which lasted a month, was a highly affectionate one. It also provided an opportunity to raise matters of concern to each. Conrad was unhappy over the meager wages he was earning at sea even as an officer. The periods of unemployment between jobs ate up whatever he managed to save. He hoped to supplement this by a business investment, and persuaded his uncle to invest several hundred pounds of the legacy from his parents in a firm of London shipping agents, Barr, Moering & Co., from whose profits he would draw a percentage.

Bobrowski, on his part, once more urged his nephew to become a British citizen. Conrad was evasive about it. He was still uncertain about his future, and even more uncertain as to whether he really wanted to break off all ties of allegiance to Poland. His uncle also suggested that Conrad write travel pieces for Polish magazines. Conrad was having fascinating experiences all over the world; he wrote Polish fluently; he had picturesque powers of observation and a colorful style; he would be adding his bit to Polish culture. To these sensible arguments, Conrad was again evasive. Something in him resisted the idea of forming intimate literary ties with his native country.

After returning to England, Conrad embarked for the East again in September, 1883, as second mate aboard the sailing ship *Riverdale*. He quarreled with the captain and quit the ship in Madras, India, in April, 1884. The one unfavorable report he ever received on his performance as a seaman came from the captain of the *Riverdale*. On the back of Conrad's certificate of discharge, there were two notations. After "character for ability," the captain wrote "very good." After "character for conduct," he put "decline," without explaining why he declined to comment on Conrad's conduct.

From Madras, Conrad took a train to Bombay in search of a new berth. Sitting on the porch of the Sailors' Home overlooking the harbor, he saw a graceful ship, with the trim lines of a yacht, sail into port. Her name was the *Narcissus*. Within a week Conrad signed on as her second mate. The journey back to Europe lasted from April to October, 1884, and was the basis of Conrad's early masterpiece *The Nigger of the 'Narcissus.'* On the actual voyage there was an ailing Negro seaman who died at sea, a titanic storm in the Atlantic which the *Narcissus* barely survived, and a number of crewmen whose names, like the name of the ship itself, Conrad did not bother changing when he came to write the novel. The second mate in the novel, however, is named Creighton, not Conrad, leaving the reader free to speculate whether they are the same.

Conrad could not be aware of it at the time, but he was meeting people and storing up experiences that were later to be used in his writing. Dominic Cervoni was the first of these, the saga of the *Palestine* the second, and the journey on the *Narcissus* the third. In due course others were to follow, a rich supply of material lived at first hand that would nourish his fiction and keep it firmly anchored in reality.

CHAPTER 6

1886

After leaving the *Narcissus,* Conrad settled down in earnest to prepare for his first mate's examination. This he took—and passed—on December 3, 1884, his twenty-seventh birthday. His examiner was a man with a reputation for toughness and unreasonableness, who asked all sorts of questions about what Conrad would do in a series of improbable emergencies at sea, each more unlikely than the one before. Since Conrad did not lack imagination himself, he managed to get through these wildly imaginary situations in good order.

Despite this success it was not until April, 1885, that he went to sea again, and then only as second mate, on the sailing ship *Tilkhurst,* bound for Singapore. The voyage was long, dull, uneventful. By the time he reached Singapore, Conrad was again thinking of leaving the merchant service and going in for something more adventurous. In a series of letters to a Polish acquaintance named Kliszewski living in Cardiff—probably his first letters written in English—he outlined a proposal to outfit a whaler and enter that more hazardous branch of seafaring. Naturally he would wait until he got his master's ticket. Conrad wanted Kliszewski's advice. Apparently it was unfavorable, for after a short time whaling dropped out of Conrad's correspondence.

The *Tilkhurst* returned to London in June, 1886, and within the next few months three things happened which made 1886 a red-letter year in Conrad's life. The first, in August, was his naturalization as a British subject. When Uncle Tadeusz learned of this, he proclaimed his eager desire "to clasp my Englishman to my breast as well as my nephew." The second event, in November, was the examination for a master's certificate. It proved the pleasantest of his professional tests. The examiner was friendly, talkative, and easygoing. Conrad was deeply gratified when he learned that he had passed. After years of effort he was now a British master mariner.

And now, perhaps, the disapproving voices that had criticized him for leaving Poland and going to sea would be stilled. Uncle Tadeusz was overjoyed. His nephew, of whose nature he had been so suspicious, had reached the top of his profession and was under the protection of a powerful empire. His future seemed assured, his ability to earn his own living no longer in doubt. Bobrowski's brother Casimir had recently died, leaving him with a fresh batch of nieces and nephews to care for. It was a profound relief to him that Conrad could at last support himself.

The third incident involved neither citizenship nor seamanship but literature. A popular magazine of the day, *Tit-Bits,* announced its annual prize story contest. Conrad wrote a story for it. Called "The Black Mate," it was his first piece of fiction and his first imaginative writing since the age of eleven when he had dashed off a play with the intriguing title "The Eyes of King John Sobieski." Conrad did not win the *Tit-Bits* prize. He put the story aside and gave it no further thought at the time. Years would pass before the idea of becoming an author would seriously enter his mind.

Yet "The Black Mate" introduced a subject to which Conrad returned throughout his writing: the man who discovers some weakness or handicap in himself, and the ways in which he tries to conceal or deny it or learn how to live with it. The "black" mate's handicap is external and accidental: he has turned prematurely gray and cannot find employment because he seems too old. He dyes his hair black and is hired, but during a storm the bottles containing the dye are smashed. He knows that soon the gray roots of his hair will be exposed. In his anxiety, he falls down a ladder and cuts his head. He wriggles out of his dilemma by pretending he has seen a ghost which made him fall and turned his hair gray. The captain is a spiritualist and swallows the story. In his later work Conrad does not permit his heroes such easy escapes. "The Black Mate" has almost no characterization, but it is by no means crudely or unprofessionally written.

What moved Conrad to write it can only be guessed at. He was always in need of money and the cash prize would have been welcome. He had little to do on shore between voyages, and writing was as good a way as any of passing the time. Literature had been a part of his earliest background, and writing came naturally to him. Possibly for any or all these reasons the impulse to try his hand at a story seized him. It was a sign of his growing assurance in English that he should have attempted something as difficult as fiction in this new language after rejecting his uncle's repeated invitation to do what was obviously easier for him, write in Polish. As a Conrad "first," the story is important. Yet it meant little to him in 1886. The *Tit-Bits* prize went to someone else, and in February, 1887, Conrad was back at sea.

In spite of the successes of 1886, however, the 1880s were on the whole not very happy for Conrad. The sea, once the glittering object of his youthful imagination, soon appeared in another light. It was romantic to be sure, but it was also wearing. The voyages had their dramatic moments: storms, breath-taking seascapes, the fresh faces and customs of Malays, Arabs, Chinese, Indians, and other peoples living on the borders of Far Eastern oceans. But for the most part the long days were endlessly, monotonously the same, with the same tasks to be done over and over. The work seemed to get physically harder with each voyage. And Conrad suffered from the absence of intellectual companionship. He began to hate the sea and, as he struggled through the backbreaking labor, to ask himself if he had been "made for such imbecilities."

How to bear up under the grinding monotony became his constant problem. It was not enough to resign himself and endure it. He could not exist simply as a dull beast in the harness of deadly routine. He had to find some meaning in his maritime life, some value over and beyond survival, if he were to continue in the profession he had so rashly embarked upon as a youth.

He had to remain at sea because to leave would be admitting his error in choosing it in the first place. But at least, he decided, he would be as fine a sailor as possible. He would execute even the most routine and commonplace details of his job with all the skill he could muster. Perfection would give meaning and dignity to his work and hence to his personal life. For Conrad, it became no longer enough to perform one's duty on a merely acceptable level: the performance had to go beyond that to perfection. Then, even the lowest or simplest kind of labor acquired a morality of its own; it became an art.

In his book of reminiscences *The Mirror of the Sea,* there is a famous passage about "the honour of labor": "The attainment of proficiency, the pushing of your skill with attention to the most delicate shades of excellence, is a matter of vital concern. But there is some-

thing beyond—a higher point, a subtle and unmistak-
able touch of love and pride beyond mere skill; almost
an inspiration which gives to all work that finish which
is almost art—which *is* art."

There was another aspect to Conrad's concern with
perfection that applied especially to life at sea. Sailing
was a hazardous occupation: the sea could become a
dangerous enemy, and there were many occasions
when only the highest skill could prevent total disaster.
The inept or irresponsible seaman, the slacker, was a
serious handicap on board ship. In Conrad's first novel
about the sea, he presents two evil characters—the two
men who do not work. One will not; the second cannot, because of illness. Together they bring the ship to
the edge of destruction. Their opposite is shown in
Ransome, the cook in the story *The Shadow-Line*.
Though Ransome has a bad heart, he strains himself to
the limit when he feels he is needed. His work is always
performed quietly, efficiently, gracefully. He embodies
the human ideal which Conrad set up for himself.

Though this devotion to an ideal made his life at sea
more bearable, it did not eliminate its difficulties.
Boredom continued to gnaw at him, undermining his
youthful spirits. This soon developed into a still deadlier
feeling, a sense of life emptiness. Even his promotions
in the merchant marine and his new citizenship did not
save him from its destructive effects. He found the sea
adventurous and boring by turns, a mixture of attitudes which, later, would nourish his art but made his
present life difficult. Conrad stated the case in *Lord*

Jim: "He knew the magic monotony of existence between sky and water . . . there is nothing more enticing, disenchanting, and enslaving than the life at sea."

In the same novel Marlow, Conrad's alert and talkative narrator, describes the coming of disillusion: "There is such magnificent vagueness in the expectations that had driven each of us to sea, such a glorious indefiniteness, such a beautiful greed of adventures that are their own and only reward! What we get— well, we won't talk of that. In no other life is the illusion more wide of reality—in no other is the beginning *all* illusion—the disenchantment more swift—the subjugation more complete."

The charm of the sea, which had attracted Conrad for so long, began to pall. The actuality of a seaman's existence was harsher than he had at first conceived, and the harshest thing about it in Conrad's case was the demoralizing tedium. Gales, typhoons, the risk of accident and death were relatively easy to endure; they at least gave him something to do and to think about. It was the dreary expectation of nothing in particular occurring, of performing the same fixed, tiring tasks over and over—the expectation prevailing most of the time—that was hard to bear. The dullness of life taxed his spirit far more than its dangers.

The arduous conditions of sea life were aggravated by loneliness. From 1878, when Conrad first arrived in England, until 1895, when his first book was published, he got to know only two people in England well. Between voyages he lived in various temporary lodgings in London, seldom returning to the same one, carrying his few personal belongings—books, papers, letters—with him wherever he went. He had only the most superficial contacts, with landladies, chambermaids, storekeepers, and waterfront officials; he was conscious all the while of the huge numbers of people around him who were oblivious of his existence. At sea, to be sure, he was not alone. But he had made no real friends among the ordinary seamen when he himself was one, or among the mates and captains after he rose to their level. In port Conrad avoided other sea captains. He was too different from them in background, personal taste, sensibility, appearance, and accent. He dressed fastidiously and retained the aristocratic manners of the Polish upper class. He was called, by no means admiringly, "the Russian Count."

The conditions of his occupation reinforced Conrad's isolation. It was true that the ship's company was a kind of organized community, but it lasted only as long as the voyage did. When the ship returned home, the crew scattered, never to be reassembled in the same form.

Conrad spent sixteen years in the British merchant marine without forming any close relationships. His letters during the 1880s are those of a man completely alone. The long voyages to Australia, Malaya, and the Dutch East Indies gave him many experiences to describe but no intimate ties with human beings. His life supplied him with materials for observation rather than with objects of love.

He suffered not only from boredom and loneliness but from uncertainty about himself. During one of his rare social encounters, on the island of Mauritius, he filled out a playful questionnaire in which he gave one revealing answer. To the question, "What trait of character would you have liked to have had bestowed upon you?" Conrad replied, "Self-confidence."

Insecurity and uncertainty about the world, and his place in it, accompanied him on his travels as fixedly as loneliness. At an age when most men begin to feel sure of themselves, Conrad felt increasingly insecure. Gradually the image of life not only as an active process but as a dangerous one took hold of his mind, and this image became the foundation stone of his art. Many of the characters in his books were to suffer from an unnerving sense of insecurity. For them the issue of survival can be reduced to a single question: Could they continue to function while convinced that at any instant some overwhelming if as yet unseen disaster might come crashing down upon them?

Bertrand Russell, who came to know Conrad well in later years, remarked that Conrad "thought of civilized and morally tolerable human life as a dangerous walk on a thin crust of barely cooled lava which at any moment might break and let the unwary sink into fiery depths." To Conrad's young mind there was already only a narrow margin between stability and chaos. Or as Jim, seeking to explain his desertion in *Lord Jim,* put it: "There was not the thickness of a sheet of paper between the right and wrong of this affair."

CHAPTER 7

Malaya

In February, 1887, Conrad accepted a berth on the sailing vessel *Highland Forest*. Three months had gone by since he had won his master's certificate, but he was unable to secure a captaincy. Time was passing, and Conrad, his money running out, was finally forced to do again what he had done before, accept a berth lower than his qualifications. He signed on the *Highland Forest* as first mate.

Its home port was Amsterdam, and there, through a severe Dutch winter, Conrad waited for the cargo to arrive from the interior. The frozen roads and the bitter cold delayed the arrival for weeks. Conrad whiled away the time in warm cafés in the center of town where, "alone in a noisy crowd," he would sit and write letters as slowly as he could: "And all the time I sat there the necessity of getting back to the ship bore heavily on my already half congealed spirits."

The ice thawed, and the cargo began to arrive. Conrad was in charge of loading operations, for the ship's captain had not yet been appointed and in fact did not appear until the night before the ship was ready to sail. He was an Englishman named John MacWhirr, whose name and appearance Conrad was to transfer with little change to the hero of his story "Typhoon." MacWhirr disapproved of the way Conrad had loaded the cargo, and was soon proved right. The *Highland Forest* rolled more violently than any sailing ship Conrad had ever been on. "There were days," he recalled in *The Mirror of the Sea,* "when nothing would keep even on the swing tables, when there was no position where you could fix yourself so as not to feel a constant strain upon all the muscles of your body. It was a wonder that the men sent aloft were not flung off the yards, the yards not flung off the masts, the masts not flung overboard."

On one such occasion a loose spar struck him on the back and knocked him to the deck. Afterward, he began complaining of mysterious aches and pains. In June the *Highland Forest* reached the port of Samarang in Java. There Conrad was examined by a doctor, who could not determine what was wrong with him but advised him to leave the ship and rest. This Conrad did on July 1, and entered a hospital in Singapore.

He wrote a vaguely alarming letter to his uncle. It naturally upset his guardian, who in a return letter expressed his concern over Conrad's health and his hope that it would not prevent him from earning his living. Conrad remained in the hospital for six weeks, long enough to respond once again to the spell cast over him by the East. The palm trees outside his window, the perfumed tropical air, the colorful mixture on the streets of Malays, Chinese, and Europeans penetrated his senses, dimming the memory of ice-bound Holland and the uncertainties of life in England. The last time he had come to Singapore, after the *Palestine* disaster, he had left almost at once for Europe. He now decided to stay in the Far East. In August he accepted the job of second mate on the S.S. *Vidar,* a steamship trading among the islands of the Malay Archipelago.

Conrad detested steamships and regarded the coming of steam as a disaster. It threatened to reduce sea voyages to mechanical operations requiring little or no character on the part of the crew. It would surely eliminate the ancient qualities of the sea: beauty, mystery, inscrutability, cruelty, promise. These were the qualities Conrad found in the universe as a whole, and he considered anything that lessened one's awareness of them as a calamity. Whenever possible, which was most of the time, he sailed before the mast where, despite the crushing labor and monotony, a man had a chance to pit his personal resources against the challenge of the sea. Steam would take all the danger and all the drama out of life in the merchant marine.

He nevertheless signed on the *Vidar,* because of his health. After his lengthy convalescence, Conrad was forced to seek an easier berth, and the work aboard a steamship was much less taxing than on a sailing ship. Moreover, the *Vidar*'s itinerary was short; her trading voyages averaged three weeks, from Singapore to the islands and back. The temperature remained more or less the same, and there were no sudden shifts in the weather. These conditions were much milder than Conrad was accustomed to, and he accepted them as essential to regaining his health.

Years later Captain Craig of the *Vidar* remembered his first meeting with Conrad and how impressed he was by the manners of his Polish second mate, whom he described as "distinguished and reserved." Getting a European officer to serve on Far Eastern trading ships was no easy matter. European seamen who stayed on in the Orient tended to "go native" or drink heavily. Conrad did neither, although the white man who went native or in other ways yielded to the seductive languor of the tropics was to be the central figure of *Almayer's Folly* and *An Outcast of the Islands,* his first two novels.

The *Vidar,* though registered as a Dutch boat and skippered by an Englishman, was owned by a wealthy Arab named Syed Mosin Bin S. Ali Jaffree—a true instance of the scrambled nature of Far Eastern commerce. It traded up and down the coasts of Celebes and Borneo, penetrating inland to settlements strung along the shores of winding rivers lined with mangrove swamps and overrun with tropical vegetation. A settlement, like Almayer's on the Pantai River or those that the *Sofala* touched at in "The End of the Tether," consisted of a ragged string of houses and shops on the river bank, flanking a landing stage. The native population was Malay; the shopowners, Arab. In each community there was usually a European or two who had married a native woman and had fallen out of his background. The trade was in rubber, resin, and gutta-percha.

Conrad made a half-dozen trips aboard the *Vidar*, It was during these voyages that he met the originals of the figures who were to populate his Malay novels: Almayer, Willems, Lingard, Jim, Babalatchi, Lakamba, and Abdulla. In Captain Craig, who liked him and enjoyed his company, he met a veteran of the island trade, expert in the habits and customs of a population richly mixed in race and religion.

Despite these fascinations, Conrad began to suffer from nervous agitation, a malaise of spirit that took the now familiar form of restlessness and boredom. On January 4, 1888, less than five months after joining her, he quit the *Vidar* at Singapore. Why he did so, he could not say exactly. He liked the *Vidar,* her captain, and the other officers. His health had certainly been restored during the months aboard her. Yet he quit with an abruptness that surprised Captain Craig and perplexed Conrad himself. In *The Shadow-Line* he was to describe a similar situation. The hero is approaching the "shadow line" that separates the "green sickness of late youth" from early maturity. Perhaps Conrad, now thirty, was passing through the same mysterious phase.

The news about his improved health pleased Uncle

Tadeusz. In a lighter mood, he made a small request in his next letter to Conrad: "Buy yourself, Brother, some good writing paper, and use good ink when you write to me. Your paper smudges and your ink smudges so that I have to work very hard before I can read your letter; and as I re-read your letters several times usually—my eyes suffer though my heart is gratified."

Upon leaving the *Vidar,* Conrad sank into depression. For a fortnight he mooned about the Sailors' Home in Singapore wondering what to do next, whether to look for another post in the Orient, go back to Europe, or simply do nothing for a while. The matter was decided for him, on the nineteenth of January, by a sudden change of fortune. The port superintendent offered him the captaincy of the barque *Otago,* presently in Bangkok. Its captain had died unexpectedly, and no replacement could be found in Bangkok. Would Conrad accept the post? If so, passage would be booked for him on a vessel leaving for Siam.

Conrad accepted at once, with an abrupt upsurge of spirits. It would be his first real command, a prospect that at once agitated and exhilarated him. His journey as passenger from Singapore to Bangkok gave him time to gather himself together for the coming test. As it turned out, he would need all his strength to survive the ordeal ahead. The *Otago's* affairs were in a mess. During the last months of his life the captain had failed to keep his accounts and neglected to report the vessel's movements to the owners. He had also been suspected of stealing the profits. In his last days he went out of his mind altogether, and spent hours in his cabin playing a violin while the *Otago* drifted aimlessly about.

When Conrad arrived, he found the ship's papers in confusion. Worse, he was faced with a first mate livid with anger because he had not been made captain, a singularly stupid second mate, and a crew that had come down with cholera. Conrad plunged into this tangle with all the energy he could muster. For a time things grew worse. The steward died of cholera. The new steward promptly proceeded to rob Conrad of his savings—more than thirty pounds—and vanished. The indignant first mate came down with the disease and was carted off to the hospital.

At last, in February, the *Otago* got under way, with the ailing first mate back on board again and the crew still enfeebled. No sooner had they left Bangkok than the wind died down and a deadly calm set in, during which Conrad discovered, while the ship idled, that his predecessor had stolen the supply of quinine and re-filled the bottles with useless white powder. Conrad fic-tionalized these dramatic misfortunes in *The Shadow-Line,* where the first mate cries out that the ship will not move because the evil spirit of the late captain is lying at the mouth of the Bangkok River, preventing the vessel from emerging into the fresh air of the open sea.

The wind did arise at last. The *Otago,* its crew still weak, took three weeks to negotiate the eight hundred miles from Bangkok to Singapore. There, a fresh crew was signed on, and the *Otago* proceeded without further mishap to its destination in Sydney, Australia, which it reached early in May, 1888. Captain Korzeniowski was now a captain in fact as well as in name.

The owners of the *Otago* were delighted with the ship's new master. He had rescued them from an awkward position and turned a losing prospect into a profit. The *Otago* continued to show a profit during the summer in coastal trade between Australian ports. Late in August it was chartered by a firm of importers on Mauritius, a large island in the Indian Ocean that had been colonized by the French, then passed into British hands after the Napoleonic Wars. The usual route to it from Melbourne and Sydney was around the southern coast of Australia. Conrad, eager for change and remembering his early geography, proposed to the owners that he be allowed to take the *Otago* on the much shorter, riskier route through Torres Strait. This was a narrow, treacherous body of water between the northern coast of Australia and the huge island of New Guinea that Captain Cook, one of Conrad's boyhood heroes, had navigated and mapped more than a century before.

The owners, as a sign of faith in their new captain, agreed, paid the extra insurance premium to cover the added risk, and wished him Godspeed. The *Otago* left Sydney in a heavy gale, sailing north instead of south. Blown by the raging southeaster, it reached the tricky waters of Torres Strait on the ninth day and turned

west into them. It then made its way through the
Arafura Sea, passed the island of Timor to the north,
and finally entered the Indian Ocean. Once there, it
was plain sailing to Mauritius, which the *Otago*
reached at the end of September.

Conrad remained on Mauritius for six weeks. A
shipper named Paul Langlois, who saw him almost
every day, set down his impressions later. He found
Conrad's conversation fascinating and his appearance
arresting: mobile features changing very rapidly from
geniality to anger, a strong chin, well-shaped mouth,
thick, well-trimmed mustache, and very large dark
eyes whose prevailing expression was dreamy melancholy. His nerves were edgy; any sudden noise would
make him jump, and he was often moody and irritable.
He dressed like a boulevard dandy: a light-colored
waistcoat under a dark jacket, well-cut trousers, an
elegant bowler hat tilted to one side, gloves, and a gold-
knobbed cane. With Conrad's excellent French and his
background as a well-born European, he might easily
have been welcomed by the permanent French resi-
dents of the island. He chose to keep largely to himself,
attending to business matters by day, writing letters,
reading, and lounging in cafés by night.

He did make friends with one family on Mauritius,
the Rénoufs. He had dinner frequently at their home,
played parlor games with them, took them out to dine
in Port Louis, the capital city, and fell in love with
Eugénie Rénouf. He proposed to her, and was sharply
taken aback to discover that she was already engaged

to be married. This was enough to send him back to the isolation of his cabin on the *Otago,* where he remained until leaving the island for good.

In December the *Otago* was back in Australia, where it resumed its coastal trading. Letters from Uncle Tadeusz began to arrive, hinting strongly that he would like to see Conrad again. He wrote that he was getting old and was anxious for his nephew to return to Europe while he was still alive.

Conrad was satisfied with his first command. It had been a success. He had sailed the *Otago* over thousands of miles of ocean with great enterprise and skill, with profit for the owners and a sense of personal achievement for himself. Under ordinary circumstances he would have stayed on, but the appeal from his uncle made it hard to continue with an easy mind. To the regret of his employers, he resigned at the beginning of April, 1889, and booked steamship passage for England.

He had been away for more than two eventful years, long enough for the *Vidar* and the *Otago* to join the *Saint-Antoine, Palestine,* and *Narcissus* as the decisive ships of his career, both as mariner and writer.

CHAPTER 8

The Congo

Conrad returned to London in June, 1889, hoping to leave for Poland at once to visit his uncle. He learned from Bobrowski, however, that this was not possible. Though the Russian government had at last acknowledged Conrad's British citizenship, permission to enter the Polish Ukraine had to be obtained from the provincial governor. It was uncertain when this would be granted. Conrad would have to wait until it arrived.

In the meantime he moved into furnished rooms in London, as he had done so often before, and began looking for the command of another ship. Again he had trouble finding one. The money he had made on the *Otago* would not last indefinitely. While waiting for a suitable vessel, he took a part-time job with Barr, Moering & Co., the warehouse firm in which he had invested capital some years before. Conrad hoped, be-

tween his savings and his earnings in this new post, to
keep going until he made a new sea connection. Meanwhile, he found himself in London for what might be
an indeterminate period. The question of what to do
with himself during his leisure, a perennial question
during Conrad's days ashore, again became acute.

One autumn morning in 1889, idling in his room in
Pimlico, Conrad took the first step toward a new life. It
was to prove a major step, though he was completely
unaware of it at the time. He began the opening page
of *Almayer's Folly,* the novel that would eventually become his first published work. What impulse moved
him to do so? Certainly not an ambition to be a writer.
"There was no vision of a printed book before me as I
sat writing at that table," he recalled in *A Personal
Record.* "Till I began to write that novel, I had written
nothing but letters [he had forgotten about "The
Black Mate"], and not very many of these. I never
made a note of a fact, of an impression or of an anecdote in my life. The conception of a planned book was
entirely outside my mental range when I sat down to
write; the ambition of being an author had never
turned up amongst these gracious imaginary existences
one creates fondly for oneself. . . ."

Later, mulling over that crucial day in his own mind,
Conrad could find no clear explanation of what moved
him to pass the time writing instead of reading, as he
had always done up till then. It was not the need for
self-expression; of that he was certain. It was not out of
boredom. He felt no more bored than usual. "The

greatest of my gifts being a consummate capacity for doing nothing, I cannot even point to boredom as a rational stimulus for taking up a pen." Perhaps, he reflected fancifully, a spell had been cast upon him by some "frivolous magician." The motive for his unexpected act remained beyond him. "The necessity which impelled me was a hidden, obscure necessity, a completely masked and unaccountable phenomenon. . . . I cannot trace it back to any mental or psychological cause which one could point out and hold to."

Wherever it came from, there he found himself with the impulse to write. He had just spent two years in the East, chiefly among Malays. The first line of the first page records the voice of Almayer's Malay wife calling him to supper. Almayer, on the shore of the river flowing past his compound, is musing on his dream of wealth and fame, on the gold mine in the interior he hopes one day to find, and on his triumphal return to Europe accompanied by his beloved, beautiful, half-caste daughter Nina. On the *Vidar* Conrad had traded in just such compounds in Borneo and Celebes and had met an actual Almayer, whose name was spelled Olmeijer. The rich sensuous prose of the novel was not only the product of Conrad's temperament. It rose out of the steaming jungles, the exotic vegetation, the perfumed air of the Far East with which both his senses and memory were crowded.

The early pages of *Almayer's Folly* filled his enforced leisure, but they did not solve his immediate problems. He still had his living to earn. It did not occur to him to earn it anywhere but at sea. However, Conrad, restless as always, was no longer satisfied with the sea routes upon which he had sailed until now. The Indian Ocean, the South Pacific, Asia, the Far East, Australia had lost some of their allure. He wanted to traverse new seas, discover new continents.

As though in answer to his searchings, a new continent began to receive public notice at that time. Early in 1890 Henry Morton Stanley, the great explorer of Africa who had found Livingstone twenty years earlier, was given a series of receptions by the grateful Belgian government. In the service of that government Stanley had traced the course of the Congo River and, as a result, the Belgians, under King Leopold II, had annexed large sections of the fabulously rich Congo territory. They did so under the banner of "bringing civilization" to the Dark Continent. They encouraged explorers, geographers, scientists of all kinds to help open up these vast new areas.

All this turned out to be window dressing. Under the cloak of the nineteenth-century ideal of raising the living standards of primitive peoples, there took place one of the most ruthless exploitations in the whole history of colonialism. Leopold himself made a tremendous personal fortune out of the Belgian Congo, as the Belgians exploited its inhabitants and looted its resources with a rapacity that knew no bounds.

Little of this was suspected in the fall of 1889. The newspapers were filled with Stanley's exploits. Africa seemed like a glamourous new world in which wonderful experiences were to be had. Adventurous men were being drawn to it from all corners of the earth. In London, Conrad felt himself pulled suddenly and powerfully into its magnetic field. The Congo was an immense river, the second longest in Africa and the artery for trade that penetrated to the very heart of the continent. River commerce required boats and officers to run them. Conrad felt himself uniquely qualified. He had a master's ticket. He could speak French fluently, essential for anyone who wished to work for the Belgians. He was not only available, but so eager to be active again that he was even willing to swallow his distaste for steam.

No sooner did the idea of going to Africa seize hold of him than he started moving heaven and earth to get a post in the Belgian Congo. Through a friend, Adolf Krieger, a London businessman connected with Barr, Moering, he secured a letter of introduction to Albert Thys, the head of the Belgian company that had a monopoly on Congo shipping. In November he traveled to Brussels and had a satisfactory interview with M. Thys. The Belgian promised him the first command available, though when that would be he did not know. Conrad thereupon returned to London and proceeded to spend the next two months in fidgety impatience. He also pecked away at *Almayer's Folly,* seven chapters of which were finished by the time he left London again.

When Uncle Tadeusz learned of Conrad's African ambition, he expressed his disapproval, suspecting it to be another of his nephew's harebrained, Korzeniowski schemes, conceived in folly and nurtured in restlessness. Anyway, Africa was no place for a man of delicate temperament, sensitive nerves, and uncertain health. The whole idea appeared a new kind of madness to him and made him more than ever anxious to see Conrad. He redoubled his efforts to secure official permission for his nephew to re-enter Russian territory. He also reminded Conrad that he had a distant cousin living in Brussels, Alexander Poradowski, who had fled from Poland during the national uprising of 1863.

At the beginning of February, 1890, plans were set for Conrad, after an absence of fifteen years, to visit his native country. He stopped off in Brussels to renew his application with M. Thys and inform him that, though he was going to Poland, he was prepared to return at once should an opening materialize. He also called on his cousin and was shocked to discover himself in the presence of a dying man. Two days later Poradowski did in fact die.

Conrad also met his cousin's wife, Mme. Marguerite Poradowska, the daughter of a distinguished French scientist, who wrote novels and fictional sketches and had acquired a small literary reputation. She took an immediate liking to her cousin-in-law, ten years younger than herself, and was fascinated, as were so many other persons who met him during the 1880s, by the experiences he had had and the adventurous tales he had to tell. He confided his African project to her. She promised to use her contacts and influence in Brussels to help him. He went on to Poland greatly encouraged.

He traveled by train through Germany, and after brief stops in Warsaw and Lublin, was met at a remote rural depot by a servant of his uncle. The man was amazed at Conrad's perfect Polish; he had expected some strange creature from another world, speaking heaven knows what unintelligible language. There followed an eight-hour journey by horse-drawn sledge through frozen fields and snowy forests to his uncle's country house in Kazimierowka, with Conrad wrapped to the eyes in a huge bearskin.

His uncle was waiting for him when he arrived and embraced him warmly. "You won't have many hours to yourself while you are staying with me, brother," he exclaimed. ("Brother" was an affectionate form of address from the speech of the Polish peasant.) In the two months that followed, Conrad had indeed little time to himself. He was besieged by visits from friends and relatives eager to see this strange prodigal returned from the far corners of the earth.

He and his uncle spent long hours together, talking over in minutest detail everything that had happened to Conrad since they last met. In turn, Bobrowski gave his nephew a precise accounting of how much money had been spent on his upbringing and how many roubles were still left in his inheritance. To put life in order was one of Bobrowski's ruling passions. Conrad greatly admired his uncle, even when not taking his advice, and was deeply grateful to him. "He was then sixty-two years old and had been for a quarter of a century the wisest, the firmest, the most indulgent of guardians, extending over me a paternal care and affection, a moral support which I seemed to feel always near me in the most distant parts of the earth."

He was soon to need that moral support in still another distant part of the earth. After further petitions to M. Thys by himself and Mme. Poradowska, Conrad left Poland at the end of April and returned to Brussels, anxious to press his application on the spot. When he got there, news arrived that one of the company's captains had been killed in a scuffle with natives. Would Conrad be willing to replace him? He would indeed.

There now ensued a feverish two weeks of preparation. He thanked his beautiful widowed cousin Marguerite warmly for her help, then rushed off to London to get ready. He traveled back and forth between England and Belgium twice, winding up his affairs, taking medical examinations, getting the necessary papers. Still breathless, he took a train from Brussels to Bordeaux, and there boarded a steamship, the *Ville de Maceio,* for the journey to Africa. When the ship stopped at Freetown, Sierra Leone, on May 22, 1890, he wrote a letter in Polish to his cousin Charles Zagorski describing his feverish preparations:

> If you only knew what a confounded lot of things I had to see to. From London to Brussels, and back again to London! And again to Brussels!

You should have seen the tin boxes and revolvers, the high boots and the touching farewells; just another handshake and just another pair of trousers!—and if you knew all the bottles of medicine and all the affectionate wishes I took away with me, you would understand in what a typhoon, cyclone, hurricane, earthquake—no!—in what a universal cataclysm, in what a fantastic atmosphere of shopping, business and sentimental leave-taking I spent two whole weeks.

The journey down the African coast was slow, with frequent stops at ports along the way. Conrad heard things from fellow passengers which began to dampen the bright picture he had of Africa. He was told that sixty per cent of the company's employees returned within six months because of bad health. Others were sent home before a year was up so they would not die in the Congo. Conrad planned to stay three years, and was alarmed to hear that only a handful of the men who went out lasted that long.

The chief source of this information was Prosper Harou, a Belgian, returning to his Congo post on the same boat with Conrad. The two men became friendly and agreed to travel upriver together. In a letter written from the *Ville de Maceio,* Conrad referred to himself wryly as "a Polish gentleman soaked in British tar," a combination which he hoped would enable him to survive the hazards of the African climate. After all, he remarked, "I can console myself by remembering that—faithful to our national traditions—I got myself into this of my own free will."

He reached Boma, capital of the Belgian Congo, on June 13, 1890, and then transferred to a small steamboat which took him to Matadi, forty miles up the Congo. At this point Conrad began keeping a diary of his experiences in Africa, his Congo diary. This, together with his letters to his uncle and Mme. Poradowska from Africa, are the chief sources of information about the nightmarish period which he now entered.

From Matadi to Kinshasa, a settlement over two hundred miles farther inland, the Congo was not fully navigable, and the only way to cover this distance was on foot. Conrad's ship, the *Florida,* was presumably waiting for him in Kinshasa. The Belgians were building a railroad from Matadi to Kinshasa. The noise of the construction half deafened Conrad while the overland expedition that would take him and Harou to their posts was being assembled.

The journey that followed was an ordeal from the start. The days were steamingly hot, the nights cold and alive with mosquitoes. The country was rough, savage, and oppressively primeval. The men tramped wearily through stretches of thick jungle. Harou suffered from fainting spells and had to be carried with great difficulty over the bad terrain. The carriers rebelled at this; many of them deserted, and the rest had to be alternately cajoled and browbeaten by Conrad to stay with the caravan.

The country seemed almost empty, but it echoed to an almost constant beating of tribal drums in the distance. There was time for Conrad to observe the passage of African birds, to recoil at the occasional decaying corpse of an African draped alongside the jungle track. Here is a typical entry from the Congo diary, dated July 7, 1890: ". . . walking along an undulating plain towards the Inkandu market on a hill. Hot, thirsty and tired. At eleven arrived on the m^{ket} place. About 200 people. No water. No camp^g place. After remaining for one hour left in search of a resting place. Row with carriers. No water. At last about 1½ P.M. camped on an exposed hill side near a muddy creek. No shade. Tent on a slope. Sun heavy. Wretched."

At Manyanga, Conrad fell ill, and the party remained there for seventeen days. More than a month after leaving Matadi, dog-tired, bone-weary, they at last reached Kinshasa. They had no sooner arrived than Conrad was given the melancholy news that the *Florida* had been badly damaged a few days before. It was being repaired, and no one could say when it would be ready.

At the same time Conrad met Camille Delcommune, the acting manager of the company. The two men took an almost instant dislike to each other, and this mutual aversion was to be another cause of Conrad's growing misery in Africa. Delcommune was a particularly unsavory specimen of the ivory hunter, in Africa to work the natives for all they were worth and rack up profits by whatever means. Conrad described him as "a common ivory-dealer with sordid instincts who considers himself a merchant though he is only a kind of African shopkeeper."

His speech was rough, his manners crude, his passion for money consuming. The abstract ideals of civilization were just so much hogwash to him. Conrad, polished, well-spoken, high-strung, a bit haughty perhaps, was just the kind of man to rub Delcommune the wrong way. When their paths crossed, Conrad had just completed a nerve-racking, two-hundred-mile trek through the jungle from Matadi. He was much touchier than usual, quicker to take offense. Under any conditions, he and Delcommune were not likely to be friends. The circumstances in which they met conspired to make them bitter enemies.

While the *Florida* was being repaired, Conrad was offered the job of first mate on another company steamship, the *Roi des Belges,* preparing for a trip up-river to Stanley Falls where an important company agent, Georges Antoine Klein, lay gravely ill. In a letter to his uncle, Conrad complained about the way the Belgians were treating him. In Brussels they had promised him a captaincy and were now more or less forcing him into a subordinate post. He thought of quitting. His uncle's reply gave him scant satisfaction. Bobrowski reminded him that he had voluntarily put himself in the hands of the Belgians, that he had gone to Africa of his own free will and against his guardian's judgment, and that breaking his contract might endanger his maritime career when he returned home.

Rather than stagnate in Kinshasa doing nothing, Conrad accepted Delcommune's offer, and presently the *Roi des Belges,* which Conrad later called "a wretched little stern-wheel steamboat," was puffing its way up the Congo. In "Heart of Darkness," the masterpiece that Conrad later wrote about his African experience, there is an eloquent description of this journey: "Going up that river was like traveling back to the earliest beginnings of the world. An empty stream, a great silence, an impenetrable forest. The air was warm, thick, heavy, sluggish. The long stretches of the waterway ran on, deserted, into the gloom of overshadowed distances. The broadening waters flowed through a mob of wooded islands; you lost your way on that river as you would in a desert . . . till you thought yourself bewitched and cut off forever from everything you had known once—somewhere—far away—in another existence perhaps."

In Stanley Falls the captain came down with fever, and even Delcommune, who was making the trip, could not prevent Conrad from becoming acting captain and bringing the *Roi des Belges* back to its base at Kinshasa. Klein, the ailing agent, died en route. The race to reach him in time, his death on the homeward journey, the significance of his personality were the starting points for the remarkable figure of Kurtz in "Heart of Darkness."

In Conrad's original handwritten manuscript of the story, the name of the African trader first appears as Klein; in later pages it is changed to Kurtz. "Imagination, not invention," Conrad wrote in *A Personal Record,* "is the supreme master of art as of life." In his fiction Conrad invented little but imagined much. As in the cases of Olmeijer-Almayer and Klein-Kurtz, he often used the physical facts of his own encounters as the scaffolding of his works. What he did with them on the imaginative side constituted his special genius.

At Kinshasa the *Florida* was being readied for its next mission: an exploration of the Kasai River country under the leadership of Alexandre Delcommune, the older brother of the company manager. Conrad's relations with Camille had now reached a virtual breaking-point. The manager spread slander among his associates about Conrad, refused to honor the contract negotiated in Brussels, and, most painfully, persuaded his brother that Conrad was unfit to command the *Florida.* This was the specific commission promised him back in Europe, captaining the vessel that would penetrate the Kasai. The Kasai, a tributary of the Congo, flows eastward through Katanga province, and it was Katanga that Delcommune was assigned to explore. Ten months were set aside for the trip. But with the manager as an immovable obstacle in his path, Conrad's career in Africa ground to a stop.

Though he had been in the Belgian Congo for scarcely five months, he had already had four separate attacks of fever and one of dysentery. The cruel behavior and naked greed of the white men depressed his spirits still further. One night, while the *Roi des Belges* was moored to the river bank, Conrad recalled his childhood boast that he would one day visit Africa. "A great melancholy descended on me. Yes, this was the very spot. But there was only the distasteful knowledge of the vilest scramble for loot that ever disfigured the history of human conscience and geographical exploration. What an end to the idealized realities of a boy's daydream!"

He began longing for the open seas, where his career had been cradled, and wrote to Mme. Poradowska begging her to inquire if the company had an opening on one of their seagoing vessels. The break with the Delcommune brothers was complete and convinced Conrad that there was no point in his remaining in the Congo any longer.

At the beginning of November, 1890, he left Kinshasa for good. The big canoe taking him to Leopoldville was manned by only half the proper number of native paddlers; it tipped over one night going around a particularly treacherous curve of the Congo. Conrad barely escaped drowning. The unfinished manuscript of *Almayer's Folly,* which accompanied him to Africa as it had to Poland, was almost lost with him.

He was back in Matadi on December 4 and, though ill again, managed to drag himself down to Boma. "I arrived at that delectable capital Boma," he recalled, "where, before the departure of the steamer which was to take me home I had the time to wish myself dead over and over again with perfect sincerity."

The African journey had been a calamity. In Europe the Belgians had promised Conrad a captaincy, but when he arrived in the Congo the promise was repudiated. He had suffered from the heat, the exhausting travel on foot through hundreds of miles of savage wilderness, the humiliating arguments with company agents, and the malaria that afflicted him. He returned home very much the worse for wear: his health badly weakened, his nerves jumpier than ever, his normal mood of melancholy intensified to the point where it was almost a full-scale sense of tragedy.

Africa profoundly altered his earlier vision of human experience. "Before the Congo, I was a mere animal," he once said. After the Congo, he was all too vulnerably human. He came to recognize the power of the primitive undercurrent in men—all men, regardless of race—and the thinness of the line between savagery and civilization. The Europeans exploited the Africans far more brutally than they did the Malays, so that Conrad's close-range view of Africa was a far greater shock to him than anything he had witnessed in the Dutch East Indies. And the Africans themselves were farther removed from Europe and the European sensibility than the peoples of the Malay Archipelago.

Before his trip to the Congo, Conrad had lived more or less on the surface of life. The African journey drove him into its dark and tragic interior. He learned to recognize that human nature itself was an explosive combination of rational and irrational, moral and amoral impulses, and it was by no means certain which would prevail at any given moment. Conrad was already acutely conscious of how dangerous the world was. He was now made aware of how dangerous men were—a more sobering realization altogether.

CHAPTER 9

Last Years at Sea

By January, 1891, Conrad was back in London, more alone and more wretched than he had ever been in his life. He felt utterly without roots, without human contacts. He felt alienated from humanity itself.

Even before his African experiences, he had begun to think that going to sea had been a mistake and that life at sea was not adventure, but endless, unremitting drudgery. Now, as a result of his African difficulties, his view of human nature itself had darkened. Men were less stable and civilized restraints less powerful than he had hitherto suspected. Violence, greed, and self-indulgence often overcame reason and self-control.

To compound his misery, his health collapsed soon after his return. He was still suffering from the ravages of malaria; now he developed gout as well and was

confined to bed with swollen hands and feet. He recalled that for weeks he lay on his back "in dismal
lodgings and expected to go out like a burnt out candle
at any moment."

His illness, his loneliness, his disillusion with the sea
and with mankind generally, worked upon his habitual
melancholy until it became a gnawing despair. Though
he had just turned thirty-three, he felt that his life was
over. "I view everything with such discouragement—
everything darkly," was one of his typical observations
to Mme. Poradowska at this time. "My nerves are
completely disordered."

His pessimism spilled over into his letters to Uncle
Tadeusz who, in turn, became alarmed. The old man's
first reaction was his usual one: the unstable Korzeniowski blood was coming out again in his nephew.
He ascribed part of Conrad's gloom "to the habit of rev-
erie which I have observed to be part of your character. It is inherited; it has always been there, in spite of
your active life." He urged Conrad to pull himself together and carry on. "I am sure that with your melancholy temperament you ought to avoid all meditations
which lead to pessimistic conclusions. I advise you to
lead a more active life than ever and to cultivate cheerful habits."

Eventually, Conrad did pull himself together. His
first concern was to restore his health. He went to a
hydropathic sanitarium near Geneva, and the baths he
took there reduced the swelling of his legs. Though
now able to walk easily, he was still not well enough to

return to sea. So, upon returning to London, he again took a part-time job as an inspector in a London warehouse. In his free time he resumed his sporadic work on *Almayer's Folly.*

More than anything, he needed someone with whom to communicate. For some months he had been corresponding with his cousin by marriage, Mme. Poradowska, who had done so much to get him his African commission. Now he began writing to her more frequently and more intimately. He poured out his fears and insecurities and inquired about her own affairs in great detail. He overpraised her rather commonplace books and deferred to her ideas, though they were conventional and ordinary. The growing closeness of their relationship alarmed Uncle Tadeusz, who warned Conrad not to let it develop into anything serious.

Conrad's health improved steadily, and in November, 1891, he went back to sea. Once again he signed on as first mate, this time on the *Torrens,* a sailing ship bound for Australia. Conrad's first trip on the *Torrens* passed without incident, and he was back in London in the summer of 1892.

In October the *Torrens* left again for Australia. On this second journey Conrad made the acquaintance of three passengers, all young Englishmen. One was a Cambridge student named W. H. Jacques to whom Conrad, after some hesitation, showed the first eight chapters of *Almayer's Folly.* This was the first time the much-traveled manuscript had been seen by anyone, and Conrad awaited his first reader's reaction with some anxiety. To his relief and secret satisfaction, Jacques liked the story and encouraged Conrad to finish it. Jacques left the *Torrens* in Australia, and Conrad never saw him again. But he never forgot him.

On the way back to England, two other passengers, John Galsworthy and Edward Sanderson, struck up a friendship with Conrad and spent many entertaining hours with him. In a letter home, Galsworthy described his new acquaintance: "The first mate is a Pole called Conrad and is a capital chap, though queer to look at; he is a man of travel and experience in many parts of the world, and has a fund of yarns on which I draw freely. He has been right up the Congo and all around Malacca and Borneo and other out of the way parts, to say nothing of a little smuggling in the days of his youth."

Later, Galsworthy elaborated on what he meant by Conrad being "queer to look at": "Very dark he looked in the burning sunlight, tanned, with a peaked brown beard, almost black hair, and dark brown eyes, over which the lids were deeply folded. He was thin, not tall, his arms very long, his shoulders broad, his head set rather forward. He spoke to me with a strong foreign accent. He seemed to me strange on an English ship."

Galsworthy went on to describe the fascination of the tales he heard from Conrad. The Polish mate seemed to have an inexhaustible supply of experiences that impressed the young man who would one day write *The Forsyte Saga.*

Others were also impressed by how foreign Conrad seemed aboard an English vessel. At that time Conrad felt himself a foreigner not simply among the English but among all men. Whatever the normal human lot may have been, Conrad in his own mind was separated from it. The *Torrens* was a pleasant ship, yet his two long voyages on it did not reconcile him to the world. Both were marked with the same monotonous toil that for years now had undermined the exotic side of sea life.

The second journey on the *Torrens* ended in July, 1893. The next month, on the urgent insistence of his uncle, Conrad traveled to Poland for another visit. This one lasted nearly two months. For a brief part of it Conrad was sick and spent five days in bed. "It is good to be ill here," he wrote to his cousin in Brussels. "My uncle looks after me as if I were a small boy." In September he was back in London seeking a job again. When none was forthcoming, he sank into a now familiar inertia, interrupted only by work on the ninth chapter of *Almayer's Folly.* He thought of the book as an escape from idleness, which he described as "the idleness of a haunted man who looks for nothing but words to capture his vision."

In November, at long last, an opening presented itself for an officer who could speak French. Conrad jumped at it. Before "black melancholy" overcame him altogether, he signed as first mate on the *Adowa,* a steamer chartered by a French company to transport emigrants to French Canada. The *Adowa* sailed for Rouen, where its passengers were assembling. It reached there early in December and anchored in the Seine.

Not a single passenger was destined to board the ship. The chartering company ran into a money shortage at this critical point, and the emigration plan was suspended. With Conrad in charge, the *Adowa* remained in Rouen through all of December and much of January, while the agents struggled to float their scheme again and the owners cast about for other clients. Conrad, drawing his wages but wishing he were doing more to earn them, patronized the cafés along the river, drawing what pleasure he could from the fact that he was spending all these tiresomely inactive weeks in the home town of Gustave Flaubert. Rouen was perhaps more universally known as the city in whose market place Joan of Arc had been burned at the stake, but it was its literary association that interested Conrad.

He had read Flaubert's famous novel *Madame Bovary,* which came out the very year he was born. On the *Torrens'* second journey he had reread it, and now in Rouen he took pleasure guessing the location of scenes in the novel. Emma Bovary, Flaubert's heroine, married a dull provincial doctor and lived a dull life in a dull town. She had romantic dreams of what life should be like and struggled to make the dreams come

true. Her attempts were pathetic, futile, and in the end
fatal to herself. For some years Conrad had been writing a novel about a man living a drab and disappointed
life in a Borneo settlement, married to a woman he despised, and sustained by a romantic dream of wealth
and rehabilitation. Almayer's attempts to realize his
dream are as pathetic and futile as Madame Bovary's,
and just as fatal to himself.

The two novels were thus remarkably alike in
theme, despite their differences in setting and social
structure. And Conrad's attitude toward Almayer was
every bit as skeptical as Flaubert's toward Emma. Yet
it was not these similarities alone that attracted Conrad
to Flaubert. It was also the Frenchman's theory of
style. Flaubert believed that there was only one perfect
way of saying anything. The perfect word, the *mot
juste,* was what he was after, and he was willing to lie
on his divan for weeks at a time—and often did—
waiting for the perfect word to come to him. *Madame
Bovary* was less than three hundred pages long, yet it
took Flaubert seven years to write.

This belief in technique, in the power of art over nature, Conrad found everywhere in France. He found it
in the absolute neatness with which the French pruned
their trees, laid out their cities, planned their lives.
Logic, order, coherence, rationality—the *how* of living
even more than the what—were the hallmarks of
French genius. It was an eighteenth-century Frenchman, Buffon, who coined the famous maxim: the style
is the man. The very nature of the French language,

with its assignment of single meanings to words, reflected the national passion for clarity and control. Madame Bovary was condemned by Flaubert as much because she was emotionally careless and managed her affairs badly as for any inherent defect in her dreams.

As a beginning writer, or rather as a man haphazardly trying his hand at writing, Conrad was oppressed by problems of construction and form. He was perfectly clear about the raw materials of his story even before he began filling the first blank page back in 1889. How to mold them into some appropriate form —there lay the mystery and the craft of fiction. Flaubert was the supreme worshipper in the cult of form, as was indeed the country that produced him. Conrad walked through the streets of Rouen conscious of the spirit of the French master. Perhaps he hoped that some of Flaubert's secrets would rub off on him at this close range.

What with these speculations, with working on his novel, and writing letters in Polish to Uncle Tadeusz and in French to Cousin Marguerite, the weeks passed, the new year came, and at last, plans to revive the emigration scheme were abandoned. Conrad was ordered to take the *Adowa* back to London. They arrived there on January 17, 1894.

When he disembarked that day, Conrad had no way of knowing that it was his last job at sea, that he would never again set foot on a vessel as a working seaman. This last of his maritime journeys was significantly foreshortened; he never really got to sea at all. Yet the

Adowa's trip to Rouen had certain Conradian features. It was an English boat named after a city in Abyssinia and chartered by the French for service to Canada, strongly suggesting the international flavor of Conrad's career. The image of Conrad, a lone caretaker on a ship moored in the middle of a busy Norman town in which he knew no one except the ghost of a former resident, lights up his social and personal position.

Though he would continue for a while to look for work at sea, his professional life as a sailor was over. He had made no ties at sea. When he left it, there was no opposition to overcome, as there had been when he left Poland. A new existence, not at sea this time but on land, was on the verge of beginning.

CHAPTER 10

1894

His first task after leaving the *Adowa* was to find a new job. The business of what he called "chasing after ships" was as vexing as ever. Shipping conditions remained uncertain, the pay was low even for officers, and vacant captaincies were rare. Conrad made almost daily visits to the Shipmasters' Society, asking the men he knew there to help him find suitable employment.

A month went by without results. In February he received a telegram from Poland with the melancholy news that his uncle had died. The shock left him deeply depressed. "My uncle died on the 11th of this month," he wrote to Mme. Poradowska, "and I feel that everything in me is dead. He seems to have taken my soul with him." Three weeks later he again expressed his anguish: "I am a little like a wild animal; I try to hide myself when I am suffering in body or mind, and right

now I am suffering in both." After ten years the grief
was still alive:

> I cannot speak of Tadeusz Bobrowski, my
> uncle, tutor and benefactor, without emotion. To
> this very day, after ten years, I still have the feel-
> ing of a terrible bereavement. He was a man of
> great character and remarkable intelligence. He
> did not understand my desire for the sea, but he
> did not oppose it on principle. In the course of my
> twenty years of wandering I saw him only four
> times, but I owe the good sides of my character to
> his affection, protection and influence.

Bobrowski had left his nephew a legacy of fifteen
thousand roubles, payable a year after his death. This
eased Conrad's concern about money, but he was still
anxious to return to sea. He kept pressing his friends
and even asked Mme. Poradowska to look into
the possibility of his becoming a pilot on the Suez
Canal.

While waiting for another berth, he resumed work
on *Almayer's Folly,* now in its final stages. His absorption in the book quickened as the end came in sight,
and his writing pace picked up. From the beginning of
March he concentrated on the novel, and on April 24,
1894, sent a letter to his cousin in Brussels wryly an-
nouncing the death of Mr. Kaspar Almayer, "which
occurred this morning at 3 A.M." Having finished the
book, he felt as though part of him were buried in it.

"Still, I am pleased," he wrote, and then added a typical qualification, "a little." Even stronger than his pleasure was his surprise "that I should be able to do it at all."

Conrad was thirty-six, an advanced age for a writer of a first novel. He felt thrilled by the idea of having written a novel but awkward too, and, conscious of its inadequacies, began revising the manuscript. He took it with him on a visit of a few days to Edward Sanderson, whom he had met aboard the *Torrens.* Sanderson's father was headmaster of a preparatory school, and Conrad asked the Sandersons to check his English. They found it remarkable for a foreigner and encouraged him to submit the book to a publisher. He worked doggedly through May, moved not only by an awareness of the novel's weaknesses but by a painful self-consciousness at following in the steps of Shakespeare, Dickens, and Flaubert, giants of literature whom he had read and admired. He was also driven by a nervous restlessness induced by unemployment.

In June the revision was finished, and Conrad cast about for a publisher. He had no contact with the literary world. Looking at publishers' advertisements in the newspapers, he came across the firm of Fisher Unwin, which was sponsoring a special series of books under the title "Pseudonym Library." The idea of having still another name pleased Conrad. Over the years he had signed himself in letters and on ships' registers in a number of ways: J. C. Korzeniowski, Conrad Korzeniowski, Konrad Korzeniowski, J. Conrad, K. N.

Korzeniowski, and J. Conrad Korzeniowski. He took a whimsical delight in playing these variations on his name.

He decided to use the pseudonym "Kamudi," from the Malay word *karmondi,* meaning rudder. He wrote it on the title page, then wrapped the manuscript in brown paper, put his return address (J. Conrad, 17 Gillingham St., S.W.) and twelve penny stamps on it, tied it between two sheets of cardboard, and wrote on one of them Unwin's address on Paternoster Row. A messenger boy was sent off with the package and presently returned to Conrad with a signed receipt. This took place on July 4, 1894.

No sooner had Conrad sent the manuscript off than he began fidgeting with anxiety. When two weeks passed with no word, he was sure something had gone wrong. He kept Mme. Poradowska informed of his hopes and fears, of his certainty that the novel would be rejected. To protect his real feelings, he pretended indifference to the manuscript's fate, which "could be no more than an inconsequential episode in my life." On July 25 he sent her a letter describing another of his nervous attacks.

My nervous disorder torments me, makes me miserable, and paralyses action, thought, everything! I ask myself, why do I exist? It is a frightful condition.

I no longer have the courage to do anything. I have hardly enough to write you. It is an effort, a frenzied dash to finish before the pen falls from my hand with the collapse of utter discouragement.

By the end of July, with still no word from Unwin, he proposed to his cousin that, as soon as the manuscript was returned, they rewrite *Almayer's Folly* in French and bring it out in France. With her reputation and literary connections, Conrad argued, this should be easy. Her name would be prominently displayed as the author, with a note indicating that the novel had been written in collaboration with "Kamudi." In the middle of August, Conrad returned to the sanitarium near Geneva, where he again took up the idea of a French collaboration, an idea to which Mme. Poradowska was apparently receptive.

His future as a writer hung in the balance at this point. Had a French collaboration with his cousin gone through, he might never again have written in English. Conrad always vigorously denied this, claiming "that if I had not written in English I would not have written at all." Yet later in the summer of 1894, discouraged by the improbability of ever being published in English, he again proposed to his cousin that they collaborate on books in French. He also informed her that he had begun another Malay story, "Two Vagabonds," which he planned to submit not to any English periodical but to the *Revue des Deux Mondes,* a famous French magazine of the day. The story bogged down and was put aside, but it was another strong indication of how Conrad, in his growing eagerness, was prepared to write in another language.

Meanwhile, there was no letup in his hunt for a new job. He even thought of leaving the British service and taking the Belgian examination for seamanship. September passed with no progress in any maritime direction, and no word from Unwin either. Conrad was now certain that there was no hope for his novel in England. He told Mme. Poradowska that as soon as the manuscript came back from Unwin, rejected obviously, he would leave it at Barr, Moering. When he went off to sea, she could send for the novel and start rewriting it in French at her leisure.

He was completely unprepared for the news when it came. On October 4, three months to the day that he had sent off *Almayer's Folly,* a letter arrived from Unwin saying that it had been accepted.

Conrad was surprised into joy, an emotion which he seldom experienced and then usually when caught off guard. Even Unwin's skimpy offer of twenty pounds (roughly a hundred dollars) did not dampen his enthusiasm. He probably would have accepted if he had been offered no money at all. Appearing in print was miraculous enough in itself. When he met Unwin four days later, the publisher pointed out the risk he was taking with an unknown author. There were dozens of novels brought out every week; *Almayer's Folly* had an obviously limited appeal; public taste was uncertain. But Conrad needed no persuading. He took the twenty pounds, reserving for himself only the rights to the French translation. When he told his cousin the good news, he added characteristically, "I need only a ship to be almost happy."

A ship was not forthcoming and—imperceptibly— he began taking root on land. He now met the first of the friends he would make as a writer. This was Edward Garnett, the reader at Unwin who had recommended *Almayer's Folly*. He was a critic with an uncanny eye for talent. Early in his career he "discovered" Conrad. Later, he was to sponsor D. H. Lawrence and others.

In November, 1894, he and Conrad were brought together by Unwin himself in a meeting at the National Liberal Club. Garnett, ten years younger than Conrad, never forgot his first impression:

> My memory is of seeing a dark-haired man, short but extremely graceful in his nervous gestures, with brilliant eyes, now narrowed and penetrating, now soft and warm, with a manner alert yet caressing. I had never seen a man before so masculinely keen yet so femininely sensitive.

The conversation among the three did not flourish. It froze altogether when Conrad, after a reference by Unwin to "his next book," remarked: "I don't expect to write again. It is likely that I shall soon be going to sea." This so chilled the publisher that he presently took himself off to another part of the room, leaving his young editor and his newest author to begin their lifelong friendship.

Conrad later recalled how Garnett, with great tact, encouraged him to continue writing:

If he had said to me, "Why not go on writing?" I should have been paralyzed. I could not have done it. But he said to me, "You have written one book. It is very good. Why not *write another?*" Do you see what a difference that made? Another? Yes, I would do that. I could do that. Many others I could not. Another I could. That is how Edward made me go on writing. That is what made me an author.

Garnett argued that the life Conrad had witnessed on sea and land must not be allowed to "vanish away into the mist and fade utterly from memory," as it surely would if Conrad did not "write another." Conrad was impressed and convinced. Garnett observed shrewdly: "It seemed to me afterward that he had come to meet me that night partly out of curiosity and partly as an author who deep down desires to be encouraged to write." If so, Garnett, by playing on Conrad's hesitations and uncertainties with great skill, was effectively encouraging.

The two men dined out together frequently. Garnett spent evenings at Conrad's lodgings on Gillingham Street where he was confronted by photographs from Poland, novels from France, and neat piles of manuscript pages in English. Before the end of the year Conrad began another novel. With some tactful nudging from Garnett, *An Outcast of the Islands* got under way.

One other significant event took place during that year. Conrad occasionally went sailing in the Thames estuary with a retired sea captain named G. F. W. Hope, with whom he had become friendly. One evening at the Hopes he was introduced to an English girl, Jessie George, to whom he was immediately attracted. The daughter of an impoverished London bookseller, she was earning her living as a typist. She was fifteen years younger than Conrad, a simple, straightforward, good-natured young woman whose tastes were domestic rather than intellectual. She was the third woman with whom Conrad became romantically involved. The first was the mysterious Rita; the second, Eugénie Rénouf to whom he had made an unsuccessful proposal of marriage on the island of Mauritius. And now Jessie George.

In less than two years they would be married.

CHAPTER 11

Marriage

Almayer's Folly came out in April, 1895. The manuscript had proved too long for the Pseudonym Library and was issued separately under the author's own name. Conrad was still known as Konrad Korzeniowski to his friends, relatives, and shipmates. He had been introduced to Jessie George as Captain Korzeniowski. But on the title page of the novel, out of consideration for English printers and readers, his name appeared as Joseph Conrad. This would one day replace Korzeniowski altogether, but for the present, Conrad had two names, to signify, as it were, his two lives. On the dedication page there appeared the inscription: To the memory of T. B. This was Conrad's tribute to Tadeusz Bobrowski, his departed uncle and benefactor.

The novel was praised by the reviewers. The *Weekly Sun* devoted seven and a half columns to it, "burying me," said Conrad, "under an avalanche of compliments." But the reading public remained indifferent, and years passed before the first printing of two thousand copies was sold out. Eighteen years and thirteen more published books were to go by before Conrad's work caught on with the general public. All the while he was highly praised by the critics. Until 1913 he was easily the most admired and least read novelist of his day.

In 1895, however, he was happily unaware of the bitter struggle for success that lay ahead. The praise heaped upon *Almayer's Folly* in the newspapers and magazines gratified him deeply. It was very pleasant to hear himself described as a new voice in English fiction and as a Kipling of the Malay Archipelago. He resumed the writing of his next novel, encouraged and stimulated. The fact that he made no money out of this first book meant nothing to him at the time. He had not written it for money but for other reasons, some so obscure that he could not have explained them to himself.

Almayer's Folly is a remarkable study of inertia, of a man who would rather dream than act. Almayer's dream is to find a gold mine reported to be somewhere upriver, return to Holland with his half-caste daughter Nina, the only human being he cares about, and reestablish himself in Dutch society.

Nothing comes of it. Almayer suffers from an acute paralysis of will which reduces his scope of action while increasing his tendency to complain. He is a protégé of Tom Lingard, a powerful white trader in the Malay Peninsula, whose peculiar pleasure it is to "arrange" and "improve" the lives of others. By dangling before Almayer's eyes the prospect of wealth, Lingard persuaded him to marry another of his protégées, a Malay girl whom he rescued in a brush with Sulu pirates and brought up as a Christian. He set the married couple up in a trading post on the Pantai River in Borneo, and there left Almayer to shift for himself.

But Almayer proves to be no match in cunning for the native Malay and Arab traders, is harassed by his wife as she relapses into native squalor, and is finally "betrayed" by his daughter who runs off with the Malay prince whose help Almayer needed to find the gold. Abandoned by everyone—wife, daughter, patron, ally—Almayer collapses, takes to opium, and dies. As a mute symbol of his failure stands Almayer's Folly, the unfinished mansion he had started to build in happier days and then abandoned. It is now being overrun by the encroaching jungle.

Through most of the novel Almayer noisily bewails his lot but is never able to rouse himself to action. He is so incredibly conscious of himself that he is blind to all else, and even his passion for his daughter comes wrapped in a hard coating of self-love. His steady descent into total sloth supplies him with the exquisite gratification of self-pity, his only substitute for the gratification of success. Conrad brilliantly exposes Almayer's inertia as one of the deadlier disguises of egotism.

Yet there are marks of uncertainty in the writing. The descriptions of the muddy river, the stifling jungle, the picturesque outbursts of nature are startling in themselves but have little to do with the lives of the characters. And with the exceptions of Almayer and Babalatchi, the one-eyed, sad-faced, wonderfully intelligent Malay politician whose talents deserve a larger setting than the Pantai backwater, the characters, both white and Malay, are curiously undeveloped.

To compensate for the sluggish and unconvincing moments, there are scenes of great poignancy—Almayer erasing his daughter's footsteps in the sand, after she runs off with her Malay lover, turning them into small mounds that look like "a line of miniature graves"—and touches of unexpected comedy, like Babalatchi and his master Lakamba listening spellbound to the strains of Verdi's opera *Il Trovatore* emerging from a hand-organ in their Borneo clearing.

For a first novel, even by an older man already well-seasoned in life, *Almayer's Folly* is a striking performance.

While basking in the critical praise that greeted his first work, Conrad was busy on his second. *An Outcast of the Islands* is another Malayan novel and deals with certain events in Almayer's settlement a dozen years before the opening of *Almayer's Folly*. Most of 1895 was taken up with the writing of this book. It was marked by his usual periodic fits of discouragement, moments of black depression when everything, including the very act of living, lost its meaning and went blank, and by lengthy letters to his new friend Garnett, enclosing bits and pieces of the new novel with requests for criticism. Conrad's gout flared up again, and he went back to Switzerland for the water cure. At irregular intervals he called on Miss George, and took her and her mother out for carriage rides or to dinner. And all the while he tried to resume his interrupted career at sea.

He had better luck finishing the novel than finding a ship. On September 17, 1895, he informed Garnett that Peter Willems, the central figure of *An Outcast of the Islands,* had been killed the day before. This was an occasion for joy: Willems' death meant that the manuscript was ready for publication. Since Conrad was now no longer an unknown beginner, Unwin offered fifty pounds and a percentage of the royalties for the rights to his second work. The offer was a modest advance over the earlier contract. Even if it had not been, Conrad would have accepted it without argument. He did not yet think of himself as a professional writer nor of literature as a source of income, though he was coming closer to it day by day. He was still Captain Korzeniowski, a marine officer temporarily between ships.

Sometime during the autumn of 1895 he made up his mind to propose to Jessie George. His courtship had been erratic, to say the least. Weeks would pass without a word from him; then he would appear suddenly with a bouquet of flowers, a hansom cab, and an abrupt invitation to spend the day together, after which he would vanish for another indefinite time.

He was a gloomy, even a morbid suitor. He kept assuring Jessie that he was ill and did not expect to recover. On the day he actually proposed, they had taken refuge from the rain in the National Gallery on Trafalgar Square. Conrad abruptly asked her to be his wife, adding that they had better get married as soon as possible since he had not long to live. He added, almost as an afterthought, that he did not intend to have children.

This would have discouraged most girls. But Jessie George was a patient, easygoing young woman of simple tastes, with no trace of Conrad's complex, highstrung nature. She was intrigued by this exotic Polish sea captain with his foreign accent, courtly manners, and uncertain moods, this "strange and courteous gentleman" as she described him. With the rain drumming outside, moved by a sudden sense of excitement and adventure, she accepted him. He got her mother's consent shortly afterward, then took Jessie on a visit to the Garnetts.

The visit was not a success. Garnett disapproved of his friend's forthcoming marriage, felt that he had too nervous a temperament for married life and that Miss George, who had no interest in literature and ideas, no visible tastes in common with Conrad, and no money of her own, was hardly a suitable choice. She had little formal education, and her origins were as plain as Conrad's were aristocratic. Conrad brushed these objections aside. He accepted Garnett as a guide in the process of writing but not on the issues of life.

Once he was formally engaged, he had to think more seriously of the future, particularly of how he was to earn his living. Two years had passed since he had been to sea, and during that time he had written two novels. It would be hard to divide himself between the two professions. Each was a demanding, full-time job. He could not hope to succeed as a writer while spending most of his time at sea, nor could he survive the uncertainties of a seaman's life if he were to break off periodically to write a book.

Some men could manage two careers at once. Conrad was not one of them. His physical and nervous ailments, as well as his own severely high standards of personal performance, made this out of the question. Now that he was assuming the responsibility of a wife, a decision as to which profession to follow was forced upon him. Was he a writer or a sea captain? Clearly, he could no longer be both.

Early in March, 1896, *An Outcast of the Islands* was published. Conrad sent a copy to a cousin in Poland, and in an accompanying letter he announced both his imminent marriage and his choice of a career: "Only literature remains to me as a means of existence," he wrote. "You understand, my dear friend, that if I have undertaken this thing, it is with a firm resolution to make a name—and in this respect I have no doubts about my success. I know what I am capable of. It is just a matter of earning money—which is something quite distinct from literary merit."

The reception of the second novel was not quite as enthusiastic as the first, but it was warm enough to confirm Conrad in his belief that he could "make a name." Whether he could support himself by writing was another matter. From the meager sale of his first two books, there was no evidence that he could. Yet he faced the uncertain prospect of this new life with the same determination he had displayed more than twenty years before when, hardly more than a boy, he left his country to become a seaman.

Side by side with his essential will to succeed lay Conrad's fascination with failure, with all the ways in which men fall short of their goals. *Almayer's Folly* is one such study. *An Outcast of the Islands,* as the title suggests, is another. Willems, the outcast, is another of Tom Lingard's protégés. Like Almayer, he can think of himself only as rich and established; like Almayer, he lacks the ability and self-discipline to achieve success. His tragedy is that of a man whose egotism outruns his talent.

We see him at first as a clerk, doing well in a Dutch firm in Macassar. He is married to a half-caste woman, has a child, and is supporting a number of her relatives who look up to him as a great man. But his ambition to rise rapidly leads him to steal a sum of money from his employer. He plans to replace it, but before he can do so, he is caught, fired, disgraced, and scorned by everyone including his hitherto mutely obedient wife. Lingard "rescues" him at this point, transports him to Almayer's settlement, and leaves him there to fend for himself.

The two white men detest each other. Bored and restless, Willems sees a beautiful Malay girl named Aissa in a jungle glade one day and is hopelessly smitten. Most of the novel deals with their love affair. Her people, anxious to learn Lingard's secret passage from the Pantai River to the sea, a secret Willems has discovered, persuade her to withhold her favors from him until he discloses it. Enslaved by his passion, he betrays his benefactor, betrays his race, and betrays his own deepest instincts. In the process, he sinks rapidly in his own estimation as well as in the eyes of others. Only Aissa is left to him. In the end, his infatuation over, he falls out of love with her only to have her kill him in a fit of jealous rage.

This second Malayan novel, a hundred pages longer than the first, is fresher and more interesting in the earlier stages of Willems' decline than the later. The sensuous jungle background is better ordered than in *Almayer's Folly,* and the exotic beat of Conrad's luxuriant prose is now more pronounced. His powers as a psychologist are again forcefully demonstrated: *An Outcast* is as fascinating a study of sexual vanity and enslavement as *Almayer's Folly* is of sloth and the freezing of the will.

Its publication was followed almost immediately by Conrad's marriage to Jessie George. The ceremony took place in London on March 24. Only the bride's mother and Conrad's two earliest friends in England, Krieger and Hope, were present. His ties to Britain, as seaman, citizen, and beginning writer, were now further strengthened by marriage to an Englishwoman.

After the ceremony, Captain Korzeniowski and his bride left for their honeymoon in Brittany.

CHAPTER 12

A New Life

Jessie Conrad's honeymoon began with an incident that she was to remember for the rest of her life. Shortly after they reached France, Conrad, as though to confirm his warnings about his imminent death, fell ill with one of his fevers. Delirious, in the grip of nightmares, he raved in Polish, a language of which Jessie did not understand a word. There she was in a foreign country, whose language she did not know, with an apparently dangerously ill husband who ranted at her in still another alien tongue.

Jessie, however, did not panic. She nursed Conrad as best she could and waited patiently for him to get better. To her great joy, his fever went away almost as suddenly as it had come. As he recovered, he stopped talking in Polish and began using English. Jessie's relief at being able to understand him again was overwhelming.

Shortly afterward there took place another incident that remained in her memory. In their hotel dining room a Frenchman mistook Jessie for Conrad's daughter, and asked Conrad's permission to pay his addresses to her. A few hot words were exchanged, then both men relapsed into an uneasy silence. "That comes of your looking such a kid," Jessie remembered Conrad saying to her.

Though she was so many years younger than Conrad, Jessie, very early in their marriage, assumed a maternal attitude toward him. She took his writing very seriously and felt it her wifely duty to "protect" him, if necessary overprotect him, against the vexations of everyday life. "His dependence upon me touched my maternal instincts," she wrote in her reminiscences, "and to the end of his life I remained a willing buffer between him and the outside world."

She thought him a genius. But she also considered him a self-centered man-baby who had to be sheltered from ordinary tasks and responsibilities. "He had been to me as much a son as husband. He claimed my care and indulgence in the same manner as the smallest infant would have done." This was a surprising view to take of a man who had risen in the difficult and exacting profession of the merchant marine to its highest post.

Their marriage worked from the start, perhaps because they were so astonishingly different from one another. Jessie may have had few literary interests, yet she provided an atmosphere in which it was possible for Conrad to work. She also typed his manuscripts, not an easy thing to do even for a professional typist like herself since Conrad's handwriting was not easy to decipher and he made many corrections. Again, when Conrad threw his early manuscripts into the wastebasket, she sensed their value, dug them out when he was not looking, and hid them in a safe place. Years later, after Conrad had acquired a reputation, they were sold to John Quinn, the American lawyer and collector, and the money the Conrads thus acquired came when they needed it most.

Some of Conrad's friends, Ford Madox Hueffer in particular, disliked Jessie intensely. The feeling proved mutual; she detested Hueffer. But whatever others may have thought of her, she and Conrad lived together happily. He described her once as "a person of simple feelings, guided by the intelligence of the heart."

Yet his marriage, successful though it was, did not cure Conrad of his melancholy. It did not rid him of his sense of loneliness and isolation. It did not make him feel more at home in England. It did, however, provide him with warm if simple companionship and build an emotional floor beneath which he could not sink.

In Brittany the newlyweds rented a house on a rocky coastal island named Ile-Grande, and there they remained until September. The house was "all kitchen downstairs and all bedroom upstairs." The islanders were "dirty and delightful and very Catholic," the men

earning their livelihood as fishermen off the Grand
Banks of Newfoundland.

When Conrad was not exploring the island on foot
or cruising along the coast in a small boat, he was busy
writing. During the late spring and summer he wrote
three short stories that he succeeded in selling to various magazines. One, "The Idiots," was set in Brittany;
a second, "An Outpost of Progress," in Africa; the
third, "The Lagoon," in Malaya. He also began work
on a third Malayan novel, *The Rescue,* dealing with
Tom Lingard as a young man long before he met Almayer and Willems. But he could not get far into it,
and after several false starts put the story away for the
next twenty years; it did not finally appear until 1920.
He began another novel, *The Sisters,* but this did not
prosper either, and on Garnett's advice put it aside for
good. Finally, just before returning to England, he began writing *The Nigger of the 'Narcissus,'* the first of
his books based on his own adventures at sea.

Back in London the Conrads found the rooms on
Gillingham Street too cramped. After some searching,
they moved into an ugly little farmhouse in Essex—
Conrad called it a "damned jerry-built rabbit hutch"
—the first of several houses they were to occupy over
the years in the countryside south of London. Here, he
settled down to his new book. After a steady pull of several months, it was finished in January, 1897.

This novel was the first of his really great works, and
with it Conrad established his genius as a writer. "By
these pages I stand or fall," he once inscribed in a copy

of the book to a friend. The story came to him easily and was written with less strain than any of his other novels. It dealt with a sea voyage, much like the one he himself had taken in 1884 on the sailing vessel *Narcissus*. One of the big scenes depicts a gale at sea which tears at the ship, threatens to capsize it, and extracts from the crew the most heroic exertions to keep afloat. Conrad's imagination reveled in the dramatic upheavals of nature. His storm scenes—later, there was another celebrated one in "Typhoon"—are among the famous descriptive passages in literature.

The story, however, is not just about the hazards of a sea journey in space, exciting though this proves to be. It is also about the hazards of a journey in mind and spirit. The crew of the *Narcissus* is assaulted by a deadly danger within its own ranks, in the shape of a seaman named Jimmy Wait, the "nigger." He dominates the crew physically: he is very tall, has a commanding presence and a deep, booming voice. He also dominates them psychologically: though very ill and confined to his bunk through most of the trip, he forces them through impudence, through appeals to their sentimental natures, through sheer power of personality, to wait on him hand and foot.

So powerful is the spell he exerts that, like a kind of dark Circe among the swine, he turns the crew into slaves. They coddle him, move him from the forecastle to a separate cabin, steal food from the galley for him, save him from drowning during the storm at the risk of their own lives, and are ready to mutiny to protect him from the captain. All the while he whines, shouts, complains, abuses them unmercifully, and exercises his malignant influence. In this he is aided by a slyly vicious crewman named Donkin, whose one aim in life is to avoid work and who looks upon Jimmy as a past master at this art.

The *Narcissus* is finally becalmed, and wallows helplessly in the trough of a windless ocean as though herself enchanted by the evil wizard aboard. Not until Jimmy's death are the crew and the vessel released. During the burial Jimmy's shroud catches on a nail, giving the impression that even in death he is reluctant to let go his hold on the ship. At last, as his body slides reluctantly into the sea, the winds come up and the *Narcissus,* rid of her deadly cargo, sails on to London, bringing to an end a nightmare journey in which all the weaknesses of the crew, all the soft and vulnerable spots in their characters have been brought to light.

To this subtle and fascinating story Conrad wrote a celebrated preface, perhaps the most famous single essay in his career. It describes the writer as one who "descends within himself, and in that lonely region of stress and strife, if he be deserving and fortunate, he finds the terms of his appeal." The writer and the fiction he produces address us through the senses. "My task," wrote Conrad, "which I am trying to achieve is, by the power of the written word to make you hear, to make you feel—it is, before all, to make you *see*. That —and no more, and it is everything."

This emphasis on the senses underlines the special

quality of Conrad's prose, drenched as it is in sense impressions, sensuous appeal, and a mastery of the physical world, the world of nature and action. Yet he is appealing not only to the visible eye but to the mind's eye. He wishes us to see inwardly as well as outwardly. His books have their double level of experience, the physical and the psychological. Conrad's art consists of binding them together into a complex whole.

The Nigger of the 'Narcissus,' preface and all, was published in installments in W. E. Henley's magazine, *The New Review,* from August through December of 1897. The book was dedicated to Garnett. With it the one-time master mariner became a master writer.

After completing his early masterpiece, Conrad wrote two more short stories, "The Return" and "Karain." Together with the three he had written in Brittany on his honeymoon, they were published in book form as *Tales of Unrest.* From his house in Essex, Conrad came to London occasionally to see Garnett and to negotiate with Unwin over the terms of the contract for *Tales of Unrest.* For the first time he dickered about money, a sign that he was at last beginning to think of himself as a professional writer. When Unwin refused to meet his terms, the author and his first publisher parted company. Conrad took his books elsewhere, but for many years they sold no better under other auspices than they had under Unwin's. Conrad continued to struggle, argue, and negotiate endlessly for better contracts.

Yet he still did not regard his new vocation as permanent. As late as 1898 he was still looking for posts at sea. In a letter written in October of that year, he declared: "I will without scruple use and abuse everybody's goodwill, influence, friendship to get back on the water. I am by no means happy on shore." He was now living on land, and his land responsibilities were becoming so increasingly involved and difficult that he looked to the sea as a means of escape.

He had originally left the land for the sea as a boy of seventeen, eager for adventure but also anxious to get out of Poland. As a grown man in his late thirties, he was coming back to the land by way of a new career —the arduous, insecure, and unpredictable career of letters. This would have been hard enough for a man of any temperament under any circumstances. Conrad was attempting it with a wife and, very soon, a son; when Jessie's two young nieces were orphaned, he assumed the responsibility for their care and education as well. He was moody and high-strung; his health was poor; and he was burdened by an abnormal tendency to gloom. It was no wonder that once again he thought of the sea as an escape.

But underneath it all lay a hard determination not merely to survive on land but to succeed. Conrad's capacity for unhappiness was equalled by his passion for experience. He may have been convinced of the folly of human hopes, but his instincts drove him to the most extraordinary efforts.

The greatest complication of his new life was caused

by money. His early novels simply did not sell. Though the critics and reviewers liked them, Conrad could not feed his family on favorable newspaper notices. The original legacy from his parents, cared for and transferred to him by his uncle, had given Conrad some capital to start with. During the 1890s he tried to increase it by business investments. But he was not a shrewd businessman. The investments failed, and his modest capital was soon gone. In 1900 Conrad described his unhappy situation: "I am a man without connections, without influence and without means. The daily subsistence is a matter of anxious thought for me. What can I do? I am already in debt to my two publishers, in arrears with my work, and know no one who could be of the slightest use."

Not being able to support his family was peculiarly galling to his pride. It was also a completely unfamiliar experience. His father and mother had come from the landed gentry of Poland, and even at the height of their troubles money was always available. In his role as guardian, Uncle Tadeusz had perpetually grumbled about Conrad's extravagance, but had always paid the young man's debts in the end. There had never been a time in Conrad's life when there had not been money back of him.

Now, however, this was no longer true. There was no one to fall back on in an emergency. One way or another his bills had to be paid through his own exertions. Some men in Conrad's situation would have tried to reduce expenses. But not Conrad. He was a

Polish gentleman, accustomed to a high standard of living. It never occurred to him to lower it. Instead, when his books did not bring in the necessary cash, he began to borrow against future earnings. He borrowed from banks, from publishers, from magazine editors, and when he finally got a literary agent, J. B. Pinker, he borrowed more and more heavily from him.

These mounting debts weighed upon his spirit, and drove him to greater and more desperate efforts at his writing desk. He began to long for popularity, not because he had any great respect for the average book buyer but because he needed popular success in order to earn a living. His hopes of returning to sea, even after he had published three novels and a volume of short stories, were nourished by the same motive. A marine officer's salary may not have provided a glamourous income but it was an income.

All this wear and tear took its toll of Conrad. It made him more nervous, gloomy, and irritable. But it also sharpened his perceptions and reinforced his will to achieve. Far from weakening or collapsing under the increasing pressure, his energies gathered renewed strength and his resolution toughened.

Conrad was faced with other problems, aside from money. He had to work his way not simply into a new profession but into a new social and personal life. He was no longer a bachelor free to do as he pleased, but a married man anchored in a fixed position. His obligations at sea had been heavy, but they came to an end with each voyage. His obligations on land were more demanding, and they continued on and on without interruption.

He had to write his books, get them accepted, deal with agents and publishers, and struggle with a language which he spoke as an outsider. There was the taxing business of finding houses to live in, settling into the English countryside, making new friends, and learning to be a husband and father at a later time in life than most men. All the while he was plagued by gout and chronic fevers, and by an unstable temperament which could get quickly overwrought but which was at the same time the instrument that produced his books.

In the old days as a seaman, he had been far more mobile. If he was fed up with the Mediterranean, he could move to the Far East. If the Orient bored him, he could switch to Africa. And if the sea as a whole became too much, he could leave it altogether for an interval on shore. In this new life on land as a married writer, he had lost his freedom of choice. He had to produce—and keep on producing—or risk having the roof cave in.

CHAPTER 13

A Pole Among Englishmen

Conrad's books were beginning to win him friends among writers in England. H. G. Wells, author of *The Time Machine, The Invisible Man,* and other celebrated works of science fiction, had reviewed *An Outcast of the Islands,* and Conrad sent him a letter of thanks. A correspondence began; from it a friendship developed, climaxed ten years later when Conrad dedicated his novel *The Secret Agent* to Wells. Conrad had sent Henry James an inscribed copy of *An Outcast of the Islands.* James returned the compliment with an autographed copy of his novel *The Spoils of Poynton.* They met, liked each other, exchanged visits, and eventually wrote essays expressing admiration for one another's work. Like Conrad, James was an expatriate who had settled in England where, in an environment very different from the America of his boyhood and youth, he struggled for success as a writer.

Conrad's first African story, "An Outpost of Progress," was published in the magazine *Cosmopolis* in the summer of 1897. One of its readers was R. B. Cunningham Grahame, who sent Conrad a long letter of appreciation. Cunningham Grahame, a part Scottish, part Spanish aristocrat five years older than Conrad, was already famous as an explorer and adventurer, fighter against political oppression, socialist revolutionary, traveler, and author of several widely read books based on his exciting personal life. He and Conrad disagreed on the issues of the day; Conrad was a conservative, Cunningham Grahame a radical, but they shared an abhorrence of the brutal European exploitation of native peoples, and both had an instinct for the heroic. They became intimate friends, and over the years exchanged long letters crowded with detailed discussions of literature and politics.

The publication of *The Nigger of the 'Narcissus'* late in 1897 brought Conrad still another admiring reader who became a close friend. This was Stephen Crane. Crane's novel *The Red Badge of Courage* had appeared in England in 1895 and was a great success. Thirteen years younger than Conrad, Crane was already famous as a writer and war correspondent. The two men, the grave, dignified Pole and the enthusiastic, outgoing young American, took to each other at once, and at their first meeting spent half the night wandering through the streets of London talking.

Stephen and Cora Crane set up house in Brede

Place, a rambling old mansion not far from the Conrads, where they entertained lavishly. The Cranes and Conrads were soon on close terms. The men talked of writing a play together. Crane, like Conrad, suffered from money difficulties, less because his works did not sell than because he lived on so extravagant a scale. He was already in the early stages of tuberculosis, from which he was to die in 1900. Conrad witnessed the growing ravages of the disease, helped Crane leave England on his final trip to the continent in search of a cure, and was deeply affected by the news of his death.

Late in 1898, while visiting Wells, Conrad met the rising young English writer Ford Madox Hueffer. Hueffer later changed his name to Ford Madox Ford, but as Hueffer he collaborated with Conrad on two novels. Ford's father was German, but he had been brought up in England and educated in France. He spoke English and French fluently, wrote with great facility, and conversed with an assurance that, while irritating many, impressed everyone. Conrad was looking for an English partner in his literary enterprises. He was not making money from his books. English still came hard to him. He wanted someone with whom to share the technical problems of his new career. Ford was an ideal choice.

What the attraction was for Ford is less easy to define. He was twenty-four, Conrad forty. Perhaps he was flattered by the invitation of an older man who, as a writer, had already won critical esteem. Perhaps he was attracted by Conrad's personality, by his fascinating background, by the compelling sense of being in the presence of someone really different. Whatever the reasons, they joined forces. Off and on for the next four years Conrad and Ford Madox Hueffer worked at the two novels published under their joint names: *The Inheritors* (1901), a political novel with science-fiction overtones, and *Romance* (1903), a straight Caribbean adventure story.

Ford was responsible for the bulk of these two books. Of particular value to Conrad were their frequent discussions, often lasting for hours, about craftsmanship and form. They talked endlessly about the technique of putting a novel together. The examples of earlier masters, chiefly French—Flaubert, Balzac, Maupassant—came up for minute dissection. The collaborators pursued the *mot juste,* the exact word, through the corridors of every page they wrote.

Both were dissatisfied with the old-fashioned way of storytelling, where events followed one another in chronological sequence. They wanted to replace this simple time sequence with an account of events as the characters responded to them. An incident might take place at one time, but a figure in the novel might not learn or think about it until later. In the new narration, the event would appear only when it was reacted to in the mind of a particular character. In this way, thought and consciousness would replace time as the mode of telling a story. Presently, Conrad was to use this new and highly modern method in his novel *Lord Jim.*

In their discussions Ford displayed an alert and

stimulating mind. Later on he was to become notable in the literary world as a novelist and editor. His relationship with Conrad was fruitful to both. He may have exaggerated his role in Conrad's life and was not always reliable in his factual recollections. Nevertheless, he was of emotional as well as literary value to Conrad at a difficult time in Conrad's career. In turn, Conrad's effect upon him was profound. "He was the noblest human being I have ever known," was Ford's extraordinary estimate of his friend.

In 1898 Conrad wrote two of his famous stories, "Youth" and "Heart of Darkness," and began another which was eventually to grow into his next novel, *Lord Jim*. In "Youth" Conrad introduced for the first time the fictional narrator named Charlie Marlow, who was to appear in three other tales. He is a captain in the British merchant service, with a passion for spinning yarns and a moral curiosity that drives him to search out in detail the meaning of every experience. As "Youth" begins, Marlow is a man of forty and is telling a group of his friends about an incident that took place twenty years earlier, when he was second mate aboard a ramshackle old sailing ship called the *Judea*. Those were the days when, as a young man, he felt he could do anything and master any situation. His experience aboard the *Judea* put this youthful conviction to the test.

With few changes, this experience follows Conrad's adventures aboard the *Palestine* in 1883. The *Judea*, like the *Palestine*, seemed to be jinxed. It sprang leaks, and had to put back to port for repairs. Then it was caught in a fierce Channel storm which almost stove in its sides. Back into dry dock for overhauling and at last to sea again. It limped down the Atlantic, painfully rounded the Cape of Good Hope, and entered the Indian Ocean. There, it crawled toward its final destination, Java, but never made it.

A mysterious, smoldering fire broke out in the hold. The crew struggled to put it out, but it persisted, until one day there was a tremendous explosion. Marlow was lifted into the air and flung violently to the deck. The captain and first mate, two very old men, as old as the *Judea* itself, were badly shaken up in the accident. The ship had to be abandoned and the crew distributed into the three lifeboats, each commanded by an officer. They made for the coast of Java as best they could.

Like Conrad when the *Palestine* went down, Marlow now had his first command: two seamen in a rickety lifeboat. Looking back, he could see the *Judea* sinking into the sea, and with it his youth and the youthful illusion that he could accomplish anything. Ahead lay an empty ocean. For days they rowed, bailing their leaky vessel, enduring burning heat and drenching rain squalls, until at last, in the dead of night, they reached a Javanese port. They tied the lifeboat to the pier and fell into an exhausted sleep. They awoke, in broad daylight, to the sight which had moved Conrad so strongly after the sinking of the *Palestine*. Staring down at them in total silence was a sea of

Malay faces, the faces of the mysterious and dazzling East, summoning Marlow to a new stage of life, marking the end of his youth.

The story is beautifully told, with just the right degree of sentimental idealization of his earlier self natural to a middle-aged man addressing a middle-aged audience.

Marlow appears a second time as the narrator of "Heart of Darkness." He is considerably older than in "Youth" and has had his fill of the Far East. He is ready for a fresh experience, and with Africa much in the news, resolves to go there. He is promised a post as captain of a Congo steamboat and goes to the Congo to take up his new job.

When he arrives, however, there are delays and vexations of one kind or another, much like those that beset Conrad on his own troubled journey to Africa in 1890. The local manager is a crude, money-grubbing ivory hunter to whom Marlow takes an instant dislike. The Africans are being brutally exploited and cruelly worked to death building a railroad for the Belgians. The heat, the flies, the brooding primitive darkness of the Congo oppress Marlow's senses and imagination. He hears of a famous company agent named Kurtz who had come to Africa with lofty liberal ideas of civilizing the heathen. The agent is now gravely ill at a station upriver, and Marlow is assigned to bring him out.

The journey in search of Kurtz is in some mysterious way a journey by Marlow into his own deeper self.

He admires Kurtz long before he sees him and feels linked with him in some obscure way. After many difficulties he finally reaches Kurtz, to discover that the agent has succumbed, in savage Africa, to his own primitive nature. He has set himself up as a white god among the Africans and has engaged in unspeakable rites, which Conrad wisely does not spell out. Kurtz's civilized self has collapsed under the pressures of Africa, but in the process he has lived with a violent intensity which, amid the horror, compels Marlow's admiration. Marlow feels himself to be a kind of Kurtz, and learns from his experience with Kurtz how far he himself can go without breaking down. It is this act of self-discovery, the central act in Conrad, which makes "Heart of Darkness" one of the significant psychological dramas of our literature.

Some of Conrad's works, like "Youth" and "Heart of Darkness," were based on his own experiences. Others came from incidents he had heard or read about. *Lord Jim,* where Marlow makes his third appearance, was derived in part from a highly publicized episode in 1880: a captain of a ship carrying pilgrims to Mecca abandoned it in a moment of danger, leaving the passengers to their fate.

Lord Jim, completed in 1900, begins with a similar incident. Jim, a young merchant marine officer in the Far East, is obsessed by the longing to be a hero. But when the ship on which he is first mate seems about to sink, he and the other officers desert. They go off in the lifeboats, leaving the passengers presumably to drown.

Miraculously, the ship does not go down, but is towed to safety by a French gunboat. Anxious to explain away what he has done, Jim gives himself up for trial, and it is at the trial that Marlow, a deeply interested spectator, sees him for the first time.

From this point on, the story is as much about the effect Jim has on the people he meets as about what happens to the man himself. The effect is nearly always disturbing. If Jim—young, handsome, English—who, as Marlow repeats throughout, seems like "one of us," is capable of such weakness and treachery, then the whole European community in the Far East must begin to question itself. Marlow himself is filled with self-doubts. Perhaps under sufficient pressure, he too would behave like Jim. The very thought that the demon of betrayal can lurk inside so promising a youth fills Marlow with dread and causes him, as Kurtz had also caused him, to look into himself.

The novel explores the whole issue of cowardice and bravery. Jim is given a chance to redeem himself on the remote Malay peninsula of Patusan. There, he rescues a local tribe from its enemies and becomes *Tuan* or Lord Jim to the Malays. Moved now by social ties and personal obligations, he acts bravely. He is the same man as before, still dreaming of heroism, but his circumstances have changed. His dream is related not just to himself but to others, and it is this new element in his life that changes his behavior. In the end the past does catch up with him, and an error of judgment on his part brings disaster to the tribe. But he atones for it by giving up his own life. He did not completely achieve his original dream, yet he came closer to it the second time than the first.

The way in which the story is told is as significant as the story itself. Marlow and a group of his sea cronies are sitting on the verandah of an Eastern hotel after supper. Marlow tells them about Jim not as the events occurred but in the zigzag, flashback manner in which Marlow heard about them from a series of eyewitnesses. He himself witnessed a few widely separated incidents. The result is a novel that flows from the minds of the characters rather than from events in the external world. This new type of psychological novel was one of Conrad's chief contributions to modern literature. Its form crystallized in his discussions with Ford and grew from his own conviction that what people thought to be true was a more decisive factor in life than the actual truth itself.

In his third appearance as Conrad's narrator, Marlow reaches his full stature. Sensitive, questioning, alert to moral overtones, he is very much the ideal Englishman. He is the Englishman Conrad imagined he himself would have been had he grown up in England. As it was, Conrad could be such an Englishman only in the imaginative pages of his fiction.

Lord Jim was serialized in *Blackwood's Magazine* and then published in book form. It added to Conrad's reputation among other writers and among a small group of discriminating readers. But its impact on the general public was no greater than his earlier works. It left his chief problems—money, worry over meeting his writing commitments, anxiety not so much about his talent but about his capacity to produce—no nearer solution.

As a seaman and writer, the Pole had settled among the English but had not yet won their hearts. With typical pessimism, he doubted that he ever would.

CHAPTER 14

The Long Pull

After finishing *Lord Jim*, Conrad took his family for a vacation. Borys, his first son, had been born in 1898 and was now two years old. The Conrads went to Belgium where, with Ford Madox Ford and his wife, they spent a fretful month on the Channel coast. No sooner had they arrived than Borys fell seriously ill with dysentery. Night after night everyone took turns sitting up with the boy. As soon as he was strong enough to be moved, they returned home.

Back at Pent Farm, the small house in Kent where the Conrads had been living for two years, Conrad settled back into an established routine: long hours of hard work at his desk, a steady stream of correspondence both personal and professional, visits with friends, chiefly other writers living in the area, and an occasional trip to London where he would lunch with Garnett or Galsworthy or some publisher negotiating for his future work.

In 1901 J. B. Pinker became his literary agent, freeing him of the need to market his books himself. Pinker also served as Conrad's banker, lending him sums of money in emergencies. Conrad had given Pinker fair warning about himself. "My method of writing is so unbusinesslike," he declared frankly, "that I don't think you could have any use for such an unsatisfactory person. I generally sell a work before it is begun, get paid when it is half done and don't do the other half till the spirit moves me. I must add that I have no control over the spirit, neither has the man who has paid the money."

The services of Pinker were a great relief to Conrad. Yet in some ways he was under a greater strain than ever. Borrowing had always injured his pride. The inability to repay his debts or fulfill his obligations was peculiarly painful. He was especially sensitive to charges that his books never repaid publishers the money they advanced him. When William Blackwood, the publisher of *Blackwood's Magazine* which had printed "Youth," "Heart of Darkness," and *Lord Jim*, informed Conrad that he had been a loss to the firm, it drew from him one of his angriest, most impassioned letters. He argued that he was not "a gifted loafer intent on living upon credulous publishers," and that he would one day come into his own:

My work shall not be an utter failure because in

its essence it is action . . . nothing but action —action felt and interpreted with an absolute truth to my sensations (which are the basis of art in literature)—action of human beings that will bleed to a prick, and are moving in a visible world. This is my creed.

But what might happen in the future could not console him for the anxieties of the present. Pinker advanced him money against the delivery of finished copy, which he felt obligated to deliver on time. But he discovered that he could not grind out his stories like sausages, that there was no connection between deadlines and art. Deadlines came and went, seldom finding him ready. This led to explanations, requests for postponement, promises that a particular work would be finished by such and such a day. Pinker would agree. Then the whole process would start all over again. "It is a fool's business to write fiction for a living" was Conrad's conclusion, but by then it was too late for him to stop. Others already depended on his exertions.

Fortunately, Pinker had an even steadier faith in Conrad's future than Conrad himself, and over the years backed this faith with outlays of cold cash. Yet there were irritations, misunderstandings, and on one occasion in 1909 a violent quarrel. Conrad was particularly slow about his novel *Under Western Eyes,* and Pinker, his patience exhausted, refused to advance any more funds until Conrad caught up to schedule. Conrad flew into a rage and threatened to throw the manuscript into the fire. But there was too much at stake on both sides for the quarrel to last. Relations were patched up and they went on as before. The incident was characteristic. Much of the time Conrad felt like a man condemned to a treadmill, writing desperately just to keep from falling hopelessly behind. "I am like a dammed paralyzed mud turtle," he once remarked. "I can't move. I can't write. I can't do anything. But I can be wretched, and, by God! I am!"

Yet there were times when the writing came more easily. He had gotten through *Lord Jim* at what for him was a good pace, and in 1901 and 1902 turned out four long stories which rank with his best. The first of these was his celebrated storm piece "Typhoon," in which Captain MacWhirr, the stolid, humorless, unimaginative captain of the *Nan-Shan,* fights a murderous gale in the China Sea and brings his ship with its cargo of terrified Chinese coolies safely to port.

The details of the storm are brilliantly rendered, as they were in *The Nigger of the 'Narcissus.'* The revelation of the story comes, however, in the unexpected discovery that beneath MacWhirr's dull surface there lies the force and will of a true hero. He is Lord Jim turned inside out, his unimpressive exterior concealing admirable qualities within.

A year after "Typhoon" came "The End of the Tether," about still another kind of man. Captain Whalley has retired from the sea after a great career in the merchant service. He is now old and slowly losing his sight, but when the daughter to whom he is devoted needs money, he invests his life savings in a shabby old vessel trading along the coast and returns to sea as its captain.

His eyesight becomes steadily worse, and this growing disability endangers the ship. But he must continue or lose his investment. A struggle goes on in him between his sense of honor as a seaman and his sense of obligation as a father. At last, he takes his own life and goes down with the ship. His daughter will be provided for by the insurance money. For Captain Whalley there is no other way out. The pace of the story is slow and stately, suited to the old age of a heroic man trapped by circumstances beyond his control.

When Conrad had nearly finished writing the story, the manuscript caught fire from an exploding lamp and burned beyond salvage. He swallowed his bitter frustration and rewrote it as best he could. In 1902 it was published as the third tale in the collection *Youth and Two Other Stories,* with "Youth" and "Heart of Darkness" as the first two. The collection dealt with the three stages in the life of man: youth, maturity, and old age. It was Conrad's most famous single group of stories.

The other works of this period were "Amy Foster" and "Falk," both love stories of a special kind. In "Amy Foster" an East European immigrant to America named Yanko Goorall is shipwrecked off the English coast. He seeks refuge in the countryside, but is greeted with suspicion and hostility. He cannot speak the language and his ways are strange. The native English are a harsh, flinty, ill-natured lot. Only a simple-minded servant girl, Amy Foster, treats him like a human being. They fall in love, marry, and have a child, but Yanko's delight in noisy singing and dancing, his foreign habits, his overflowing emotions are so different from the severe, restrained manners of the region that they isolate him still further and at last chill even Amy's simple heart. She leaves him. Utterly alone, he wilts, falls ill, and dies. This powerful story is at once an account of love flourishing under bizarre circumstances and Conrad's critical view of the less attractive side of his adopted land.

"Falk" is also a love story, and in its own way just as strange. Falk, a Swedish tugboat captain on a river in the Far East, is suffering from the memory of a hideous deed he committed years before: starving on a derelict ship, he saved his own life by becoming a cannibal. He has now fallen in love, but feels he cannot declare his love without confessing what he has done. The girl he loves, a strapping young German, does not seem to mind, though it is hard to tell since neither she nor Falk speaks a word of each other's language. But her uncle, on whose boat she is living, is horrified. His horror, however, is finally overcome, and the two lovers are joined. Aside from Falk's strange problem, the man and woman here are like their counterparts in "Amy Foster": they can barely talk to each other. Yet Conrad achieves something extraordinary in convincing us that love can bloom in such unlikely situations.

Typhoon and Other Stories, which included "Amy

Foster" and "Falk," appeared as a book in 1903. At the beginning of that year Conrad plunged into his next novel, the longest and most ambitious of his career. This was *Nostromo,* a work with which he wrestled for twenty long months in 1903 and 1904, months of hard, unremitting, nerve-racking labor. He despaired a hundred times of its ever coming to an end. "I suppose I went to bed sometimes, and got up the same number of times. Yes, I suppose I slept, and ate the food put before me. . . . Indeed, it seemed to me that I had been sitting at that table surrounded by the litter of a desperate fray for days and nights on end."

It was Jessie who put the food before him day after day and waited patiently through the long months for the book to be finished. Even a serious accident suffered early in 1904 failed to blight her good humor. She fell in a London street and injured her knee badly. In the years that followed, she underwent a series of operations. These did little good, and she remained partly crippled for the rest of her life. Yet she never lost her temper or her essential cheerfulness. She could not help Conrad in his art, but she did create a climate in which it flourished.

It did not flourish easily. Halfway through *Nostromo,* Conrad wrote to Galsworthy: "No work done. No spring left to grapple with it. Everything looks black. I feel myself losing my footing in deep waters. They are lapping about my hips." And when the novel was at last completed, he announced the fact to Garnett with his usual self-irony: "I drop you these lines just to say that Nostromo is finished; a fact upon which my friends may congratulate me as upon a recovery from a dangerous illness."

Nostromo was a new departure for Conrad in a number of ways. Its setting was not the Malay Archipelago or Africa but South America. Its plot dealt primarily with revolutionary politics. Its aim was to create nothing less than a whole society, complete with classes, professions, economic processes, political institutions, rival interests, and a historical past.

Conrad's brief personal contact with South America took place in 1876 when, during his gunrunning expedition with Dominic Cervoni, he spent a few hours on the Venezuelan coast. He had learned a good deal from the memoirs of travelers to South America, and made up the rest out of his own imagination. The theme of politics had already appeared in his earlier work. The Arabs and Malays surrounding Almayer and Willems are politicians to the core. On Patusan, Jim is knee-deep in political intrigue.

But *Nostromo* is filled with a different kind of politics, the politics of revolution. It is the overthrow of institutions, not the mere jockeying for status or jobs, that is at stake. *Nostromo* is the first of three great novels dealing with political revolution which Conrad now wrote in succession. The other two are *The Secret Agent* and *Under Western Eyes*. Conrad's interest in politics began with the very air he breathed in his father's house; the politics of violence was intimately illustrated in Poland's periodic revolts against the

Russians. Conrad's later experiences with the Carlist rebellion, with gunrunning in Latin America, with Malay intrigue during his years in the Orient, with the Belgian occupation of the Congo, made the political process even more concretely familiar to him.

Conrad's own political views were conservative. He was an aristocrat rather than a democrat, an individualist rather than an advocate of social action. He did not believe in progress as a law of history. He approached human nature as something to be cautiously investigated rather than blindly and joyously released. He disliked reformers and socialists, felt that revolutions did more harm than good and that it was useless to change political institutions as long as the human heart remained unchanged.

At the same time he detested colonial exploitation, and in his work frequently criticized the several forms of it present in his day. He saw very clearly that exploitation was not limited to one or another nation. The Belgians, Germans, French, Dutch, Spanish, Russians, Americans, and even his beloved British took their turn at it. Conrad admired the British Empire as the great force working for world order at a time of growing unrest, but even the British were not free from his criticism, as "Amy Foster" proved on the human side and *Nostromo* on the political.

To present the revolutionary process in operation, Conrad created in *Nostromo* the fictitious South American republic of Costaguana. He crowded into the story as much of humanity as it could hold: Latins and

Anglo-Saxons, Christians and Jews, Negroes and whites, Italians, Spaniards, English, Americans, Indians, cultivated aristocrats and illiterate peasants. This novel, he said, was his widest canvas. A whole world comes to life before our eyes in leisurely, painstaking detail.

At the center of that world, at the heart of Costaguana, is the San Tomé silver mine. The mine attracts foreign investments and supplies the yeast for the ferment of revolution. It thrusts a primitive, backward, semifeudal community directly into the path of late nineteenth-century industrialism. Without the mine, Costaguana would be only another obscure little South American republic dozing away in a remote backwater. With it, the land is a volcanic hotbed of social and political instability.

There are two parties in Costaguana, and the struggle between them supplies the main action of the story. In office at the start are the moderate liberals, who lease the silver mine to foreign investors and are supported by them. Opposing the party in power are the nationalists, who want to throw out the foreigners and run the mine themselves. During the novel the nationalists foment a revolt, overthrow the moderates, rule for a time, and are in turn overthrown by the moderates staging a comeback.

The individual characters are for the most part in the camp of the moderates. Charles Gould, an English engineer, runs the mine. His wife helps him, as does their friend Dr. Monygham. Nostromo, chief of the

longshoremen, the "magnificent capataz de cargadores," is also in the service of the moderates. Even
Martin Decoud, a cynical Costaguana journalist who
sees through the pretensions of both parties, throws in
his lot with the moderates and their foreign friends.

Each is victimized by the upheavals in Costaguana.
Gould is obsessed with the idea of working the mine;
he frantically tries to save a huge silver treasure threatened by the rebels, and fails. Mrs. Gould sees her marriage wasting away as a result of her husband's unhappy obsession with the mine. Dr. Monygham, whose
one sustaining emotion is his secret love for Mrs.
Gould, suffers at her unhappiness. Nostromo feels his
whole identity as "nostre uomo," our man, undermined by the downfall of the regime to which he has
devoted himself. And Decoud commits suicide when,
after the cause which he has supported is lost, he finds
himself in terrifying isolation on a lonely island.

In *Lord Jim* society on Patusan gives the hero
moral support and psychological strength; but society
in Costaguana proves treacherous and weakens the
characters throughout. Conrad once advised Galsworthy to be skeptical about every idea that went into
his work. Skepticism was the principle to which Conrad was dedicated. Afraid that he might have been
taken in by the claims of society in *Lord Jim,* Conrad
took another hard look at society in *Nostromo.* The result is a reversal of the earlier novel. In *Lord Jim* men
relying solely on themselves fail and must turn to
others to survive. In *Nostromo,* by contrast, men rely-

ing on society are betrayed and must fall back on their own inner resources to survive.

Both political parties in Costaguana are pitilessly examined. The moderates commit the great error of subordinating men to money. The nationalists rely on the native peasants, whom Conrad regarded as incapable of governing themselves. Giving them arms, he felt, was like putting rifles in the hands of children.

Among the major figures in *Nostromo* only Mrs. Gould survives intact. This warm, dignified woman survives the slow decay of her marriage and the rapid decay of the country through a strength of character, a serenity of spirit that touch and redeem those around her. She has been deeply injured but carries on with grace. Her first name, Emilia, resembles the first name of Conrad's mother, Evelina. It is not inconceivable that in creating this memorable figure Conrad was paying a final tribute to the patient, enduring woman who shared her husband's harsh exile and helped redeem it by the dignity and fortitude of her presence.

The massive novel was at last finished. Nothing quite like it had been seen in English literature. Conrad himself took a pessimistic view of its prospects. Before even starting it, he had written to Garnett: "The *Outcast* is a heap of sand, the *Nigger* a splash of water, *Jim* a lump of clay. A stone, I suppose, will be my next gift to impatient mankind—" As far as "impatient mankind" was concerned, a stone it turned out to be. There was no stampede to the bookstalls to buy *Nos-*

tromo. Public indifference was as massive as the novel itself.

Conrad was now at the height of his powers and achievement as an artist, yet seemed as far away as ever from finding the wide audience he longed to reach.

CHAPTER 15

The Underground Life

The ordeal of writing *Nostromo* had made Conrad jumpier than usual and kept him away from company. "If I did better work, more of it and a little easier you would see me often enough," he explained apologetically. "As it is I am shy of inflicting myself upon my friends. I go about oppressed, severely irritated against my work, never free from it, never satisfied with it. Not a man of profit or pleasure for his friends." Even the sheer relief of coming to the end of a long, difficult enterprise was denied him. "The strain has been too great," he said, "has lasted too long."

At the beginning of 1905, with *Nostromo* behind him, Conrad took his wife and son to Capri for a long holiday. They did not have a happy time of it. The weather was cold and rainy, and Conrad came down with the flu. When he recovered, he had trouble sleeping. He was able to write very little. Jessie spent most of her time in a wheelchair recovering from an operation on her injured knee. The one happy event was the news that King Edward VII had awarded him five hundred pounds for his services to literature. Some fifteen years later, Edward's son George V was to offer him a knighthood, which Conrad turned down. But he could not afford to turn down money. Indeed, he was delighted to get it.

This was the second time Conrad had been given such an award. In 1902 the Royal Literary Fund had granted him three hundred pounds; in 1908 two hundred additional pounds would come from the same source. All these grants were inspired by the efforts of Conrad's friends. There was little they could do to get readers for Conrad, but by praising him in the right places they were able to get money for him from official and semiofficial quarters. On each occasion, the money went to pay his more serious debts.

In the spring of 1905, while still in Italy, Conrad wrote an essay "Autocracy and War," prompted by the Russo-Japanese War then in progress. He described the distasteful aspects of the czarist regime, but the essay was chiefly a warning against the ambitions and might of Germany, now reunited and eager to become a world power. Back home in England, he wrote a number of the sea sketches presently to be published as *The Mirror of the Sea.* These included an account of his youthful adventures with the *Tremolino,* a tribute to Lord Nelson, recollections of shipmates and of cap-

tains he had served under, and reflections on the sea
—the fickle, fascinating, unconquerable element, as he
called it, where he had spent his years from sixteen to
thirty-six.

In the fall of 1905 Borys, now seven years old, became ill with scarlet fever, while his father came down
with another seizure of gout. When both had recovered, Conrad began work on his next volume of short
stories, *A Set of Six.* Of the half-dozen tales in the collection, three were of special interest. "The Duel," a
lengthy anecdote about two of Napoleon's officers
who fight a long series of duels with each other, reflected Conrad's absorption in the Napoleonic era.
Napoleon had played a great role in the imagination
and history of Poland in the nineteenth century. Conrad's ancestors on both sides had fought in Napoleon's
armies. He did research off and on for a novel with a
Napoleonic background, though he never got around
to writing it until the last year of his life. This novel,
Suspense, was unfinished at his death.

Two of the other stories in *A Set of Six,* "The Anarchist" and "The Informer," dealt with the underground anarchist movement which had sworn to
overthrow the governments of Europe. The stories
were preliminary to Conrad's next novel, *The Secret
Agent,* begun early in 1906, a large-scale treatment of
anarchism in London. Conrad's knowledge of the
actual revolutionary world was scanty. "You well
know that anarchy and anarchists are outside my experience," he wrote to Mme. Poradowska. "I know al-

most nothing of the philosophy, and nothing at all of the men. I created this out of whole cloth."

What little he did know came from a casual reading of newspapers and from conversations with Ford Madox Ford about the anarchists in Soho. An actual attempt to bomb Greenwich Observatory was the basis of a similar incident in the novel. A retired Scotland Yard inspector had recently published his memoirs; reading them gave Conrad the idea for the character of the Assistant Commissioner. There was little he could use from his memory of Polish politics. His father, he always insisted, had been not a revolutionist but a nationalist. He had not wanted to overthrow the structure of Polish society or, like the anarchists, overthrow all government, but only throw the Russians out and restore Poland's independence.

After *The Secret Agent* appeared, Conrad received letters from readers congratulating him on the accuracy of his anarchist portraits. Conrad was deeply pleased. He ascribed this success to the power of imagination, to his concern with his characters as human beings rather than as examples of political doctrine. "I have no doubt," he remarked in his Author's Note to the novel, "that there had been moments in the writing of the book when I was an extreme revolutionist. I don't say this to boast. I was simply attending to my business. I could not have done otherwise."

His imagination, to be sure, made up for the lack of direct contact with anarchism. It was nevertheless stimulated, at least indirectly, by a personal knowledge of something which he did share with the anarchists—the underground life. His father had been a member of the Polish underground, and he had shared his father's punishment for underground activities. Poland itself was one vast underground in the years when Conrad was growing up. Even though it was the underground of nationalism rather than of anarchism, the psychology of underground life remains much the same regardless of the doctrine involved.

One aspect of that psychology is the sense of being cut off or set apart. As a foreigner through most of his life, Conrad was intimately familiar with this sense of "differentness." In France he had been a newcomer from his native Poland. In the Far East he had been called "the Russian Count" by his fellow officers in the merchant marine. In England he remained incurably foreign. He spoke English with a heavy accent, which his wife claimed grew more marked the longer he lived in England. This was reinforced by his looks, gestures, and general appearance. Though he lived in England for more than thirty years, he was never taken for an Englishman, not even at the height of his fame as a novelist in English. In this sense he was an outsider, living in a kind of underground, the exile's underground.

As an artist, too, he lived apart in another kind of underground. The strain of writing in an acquired language was increased in Conrad's case by his balky temperament. He was desperately afraid of running dry, of becoming sterile: "I haven't been able to write and felt like cutting my throat. Not a ghost of a notion in my head, not a sentence under the pen." He compared his art to quarrying in the depths of a coal mine. "I had to work like a coal miner in his pit quarrying all my sentences out of a black night," he wrote to Garnett in 1908. And in a letter to Arthur Symons: "I have been quarrying my English out of a black night, working like a coal miner in his pit. For fourteen years now I have been living as if in a cave without echoes."

This "cave without echoes," as he put it, was his own tormented creative life. Into it he withdrew on each working day and there, cut off from the rest of the world, he struggled with the act of creation, and in a medium, English, which as late as 1907 he still described as "a foreign language to me, requiring an immense effort to handle." He was surrounded, not by real people, but by the characters of his novels. The isolation chamber of his imagination was another level of existence, a subterranean level, and it was here that Conrad absorbed finally the atmosphere of underground existence. This direct experience with the double life was his key to *The Secret Agent* and *Under Western Eyes,* novels concerned with the double lives of men and women committed to conspiratorial politics. Conrad may not have been a student of the anarchist movement, but he understood its psychology from lessons drawn from his own deepest self.

Adolf Verloc, the pivotal figure of *The Secret Agent,* is an Alsatian living in London, married to an Englishwoman much younger than himself. He is lead-ing not just a double life but a triple and even a quadruple one. On the surface, he is a shopkeeper in Soho. But secretly, he is an anarchist taking part in anarchist plots. More secretly, he is a police informer, buying his own safety by keeping the London police informed of what the anarchists are up to. More secretly still, he is an agent of the Russian Embassy, selling anarchist secrets to the czar and serving as a tool of Russian interests.

This existence on four different levels would drive most men out of their minds. But Verloc, fat, lazy, slow-moving, is at ease in all of them. He is a home-loving man who likes his comforts and wants to keep his regular routine undisturbed. His activities may not be respectable, but he himself is the very acme of respectability. This portrait of a cautious, prudent man who becomes a revolutionary, a stool pigeon, and a spy while remaining all the while the soul of conventionality is one of Conrad's most brilliant creations.

There are other striking figures in the novel. Verloc's wife, Winnie, has a placid and unruffled outward manner, yet buried within is a current of deep, violent feeling which, when aroused, turns her into a murderess. She marries Verloc not out of love but because she thinks he will take care of the one person in the world she really loves, her half-witted brother Stevie. In contrast to his sister, Stevie's feelings are all on the surface. He cannot stand violence or pain of any kind, and even the common sight of a cabman flogging his horse sends him into a nervous tantrum.

There is the Professor, who goes about London with a bomb in his pocket. He has informed the police that, if arrested, he will detonate it, killing himself of course but killing everyone else within sixty yards, including the officers who have come to arrest him. Needless to say, the police give him a wide berth. His chief enemy is Inspector Heat, who is generally on good terms with thieves but cannot understand the anarchists. Conrad has a famous passage on the kinship between police and criminals, both of whom accept the same set of rules and therefore understand each other. The anarchists do not accept the rules, so that Inspector Heat does not know how to deal with them and remains in a perpetual state of rage and frustration.

The action of *The Secret Agent* begins with Mr. Vladimir, the Russian attaché, ordering Verloc to blow up Greenwich Observatory. This, he hopes, will so outrage British public opinion that the anarchists will be driven out of the country. Verloc is unhappy over the assignment but is forced to carry it out. Reluctant to do it himself, he instructs his trusting young brother-in-law to place a suitcase in Greenwich Observatory. Unknown to Stevie, the case contains a bomb. On the way, the young man stumbles, drops the bomb, and is blown to pieces. When Winnie learns of her brother's death, she kills her husband and flees from the scene of the crime in the hope of escaping the gallows, but in a moment of despair commits suicide.

The novel is a tragedy of misunderstandings. Nobody understands anyone else. Winnie has no idea of what Verloc is doing, and Verloc is astonished when his wife suddenly assaults him with a kitchen knife. Inspector Heat and his superior, the Assistant Commissioner, are at cross purposes, and the anarchists, though bound together in a common cause, either quarrel incessantly or are ignorant of one another's motives. In a sense, all the figures are secret agents, secret from one another.

And all of them are locked up in a London which is gloomy, rainy, and overwhelming, which resembles an "aquarium from which the water had been run off." Images of drowning and darkness pervade the novel, and irony courses through it like a river of acid. The book is not only one of Conrad's most powerful; it is also one of his harshest. It takes a cynical view of its shabby lot of revolutionaries, a pessimistic view of human relationships, and a nightmare view of London and the life of man in a great modern city.

Conrad's situation when the novel was being written helps explain it. The public indifference to *Nostromo* had been especially disheartening to him. He had secretly counted on its success after the failure of his earlier novels. It was in a state of bitter disappointment that he began *The Secret Agent*.

Mrs. Conrad, who was expecting her second child at the time, described his manner during the writing: "As I did not know in the least what the book was about, I could not account to myself for the grimly ironic expression I used often to catch on his face. Could it have reference to the expected baby? No! It was only a reflection of the tone of the book's." The Galsworthys had loaned the Conrads their London house, and there, in August, 1906, Conrad's second son was born. He was named John Alexander in honor of John Galsworthy, on whose premises he had been ushered into the world.

Eager for another stay abroad and hoping this time for better luck, Conrad took his family to southern France at the beginning of 1907. But a month after they arrived in Montpellier, Borys came down with acute bronchitis. The doctor took a grave view of his condition, hinted at the possibility of tuberculosis, and recommended that he be taken to Switzerland for treatment. In great anxiety, the Conrads moved to Geneva. There, Borys' condition grew worse, and John came down with whooping cough. At one point both their lives were despaired of. It was in Geneva, surrounded by these grim anxieties in the summer of 1907, that Conrad added to, revised, and finally finished *The Secret Agent*. It stands as a monument to Conrad's stark view of life at a somber moment of his career.

After several crises his two sons recovered from their illnesses, and the Conrads returned to England, considerably the worse for wear. Pent Farm was now too small for them, and they looked about for larger quarters while Conrad began adjusting himself to the increased demands of fatherhood. As a father, Conrad was enthusiastic and irritable by turns. He was devoted to his sons, but when at work or not feeling well, which was much of the time, he wanted them out of sight. During all the family emergencies, Jessie Conrad somehow managed to protect her husband from domestic frictions without being, at the same time, unfair to her sons. Her task was made harder by the fact that, as a writer, Conrad was home all the time. He never seemed to get over his surprise at being a father at all. He used to complain, half-jokingly, that his two sons (born eight years apart) each entered the world on a Tuesday, his best working day, thus wrecking his weekly schedule.

In 1908 Conrad began work on the third and last of his novels on politics and revolution, *Under Western Eyes.* He had interrupted the writing of *Nostromo,* the first of the series, to turn out the sketches that grew into what he called "a volume of impressions and memories," *The Mirror of the Sea.* Late in 1908, at Ford's invitation, he interrupted *Under Western Eyes* to write the individual chapters of his second personal memoir, published in book form as *A Personal Record* in 1912.

Ford had become editor of a new magazine, *The English Review,* and asked Conrad for contributions. Conrad agreed. The two men had been close friends for ten years. Long after they had ceased writing novels together, Ford had continued to help Conrad by his stimulating conversation, taking dictation when the older man was disabled by gout, supplying information about anarchist politics of which he had some first-hand knowledge, and even writing brief fragments of

Nostromo when Conrad bogged down. The two families went on vacations together. Their children played together, and despite the coolness between Ford and Mrs. Conrad, intimacy between the households continued.

A Personal Record was Conrad's second fragment of autobiography. In it he described how he first went to sea and how he came to write his first book. By putting his two careers together, he hoped to show the "subtle accord" that existed between them. The tone was impersonal, the style restrained. Conrad disliked confessions and autobiographies that told all. He wished to describe his experiences rather than bare his soul.

After seven installments had appeared in *The English Review,* Conrad felt unable to write any others. Ford urged him to, claiming Conrad had promised him more. A quarrel broke out, not one of those explosive, bloodletting quarrels that turn friends into enemies, but real enough to end the closeness between the two men. There was never any open break, but after the summer of 1909 contacts between them dwindled. The original warmth was never restored.

Conrad's discouragement at this time can be judged by his bitter remark to Ada Galsworthy that in all of 1908, with thirteen books to his credit, his royalties amounted to less than five pounds. He owed Pinker alone more than fifteen hundred pounds, and though the largest, it was by no means his only debt.

He took out some of his bitterness on the reading public. "You will realize the inconceivable stupidity of the common reader—the man who forks out the half crown." But he remained no less anxious to win the favor of this inconceivably stupid common reader. He needed him to pay his debts. He also needed him to prove that his choice of writing as a career, that in fact the whole course of his life since his violently criticized departure from Poland had not been a colossal mistake.

So on he went with his writing. He was now fifty years old and had indeed no other choice. Conrad's capacity for suffering was almost as great as his creative capacity, the two being closely linked. In his letters he complained about his lot continually, but he bore it and bore up under it. And, as *Under Western Eyes* was soon to prove, his work as a writer showed no signs of faltering.

CHAPTER 16

Conrad's Russia

A curious fact about Conrad's career as a novelist is that he wrote practically nothing about Poland. It was his native country. He spoke and wrote Polish fluently throughout his life, and kept in close touch with his relatives back home. The fate of Poland as a nation remained close to his heart. Jessie Conrad recalled that in his later years he spoke more than once of leaving England and returning to Poland to live. Yet, in the whole of his work, there is only a single Pole to be found—the vaguely drawn nobleman in the story "Prince Roman."

There is no shortage of figures from other countries. Germans and Russians appear frequently, as do English, Italians, Dutch, and French. There are Congolese and Ruthenians, Chinese and Malays. In *Nostromo,* the melting pot among Conrad's novels, there is even an American. But no Poles. Conrad's studious avoidance of his native land in his art is one of the strange phenomena of his professional life.

Whatever inhibitions he may have felt about including Poland, he had none with regard to her traditional enemies, Germany and Russia. Three of his most vivid characters are Germans. One is the captain of the *Patna* in *Lord Jim,* the first officer to abandon ship. He is a man of vulgar manners and ferocious conceit, whose one exclamation whenever anything goes wrong is, "I shpit on it." A second is the hotelkeeper Schomberg, who plays a prominent role in the later novel *Victory*. He too is a man of overwhelming vanity. He hates and envies men of better quality than himself, and seeks to drag them down. Meanness and sly intelligence mark all his actions.

To Conrad, these two represent Prussian aggressiveness. His third German is Captain Hermann in "Falk," a good-natured, thick-skinned man of very limited emotional range. He embodies, to his author, German mediocrity. Mediocrity wedded to belligerence and self-love make up the German image in Conrad's view.

His response to Russia far exceeded his feelings about Germany. Russia was the immediate oppressor. She had enslaved the major part of Poland and sent Conrad's father into bleak exile. She had tried by every means to destroy Polish culture and to Russianize Poland. The Russians were the enemy of everything Conrad valued as a Pole. He described the Russian empire as a blind despotism that crushed its subjects, a country that had never done "a single generous deed" or performed any service for humanity.

Conrad was sensitive about being called a Slav, and always insisted that Poland was a Latin, not a Slavic, country, Western in her ties, not Eastern. He boycotted Russia and everything Russian on all occasions. Let a Russian appear on the program of a meeting in England, and Conrad would refuse to be present. He would turn down magazine offers if a Russian were in any way involved. During Ford Madox Ford's last months as editor of *The English Review,* the magazine acquired a new owner, thought by Conrad to be of Russian origin. He refused to contribute further, intensifying his quarrel with Ford.

He even disliked the great Russian novelists of the nineteenth century, whom he read in Mrs. Constance Garnett's famous translations. Tolstoy was too mystical to suit him, and Dostoevsky he positively loathed. "He is too Russian for me. It [*The Brothers Karamazov*] sounds to me like some fierce mouthings from prehistoric ages." Yet he confessed to admiring Dostoevsky's power and was perhaps more influenced by him than he realized. Thomas Mann believed Stevie, in *The Secret Agent,* to be modeled on Prince Myshkin of *The Idiot.* And Razumov, the hero of *Under Western Eyes,* goes through mental debates with himself that remind one of Raskolnikov in Dostoevsky's *Crime and Punishment.*

The huge gloomy weight of Russia oppressed Conrad's imagination. He was repelled and horrified, yet also fascinated to the point of obsession. This obsession led him to create a whole novel about Russians, though he wrote but one minor short story about Poles. In *Under Western Eyes,* his last really great novel, Conrad worked off some of his explosive feelings about Russia. It served as an outlet for his violent dislike of his country's powerful enemy.

The hero of *Under Western Eyes* is Razumov, whose name comes from the Russian and Polish word *razum,* reason; Razumov reasons everything out, and often reasons it out of shape. The novel begins in St. Petersburg with a brilliant piece of psychological irony. Razumov, a student at the university, is self-centered and aloof, interested only in his own career. The other students mistakenly interpret his detachment as idealism and moral strength. He acquires an undeserved reputation as someone who can be relied upon.

When Haldin, an anarchist student, throws a bomb at a government minister, killing him, he asks Razumov to help him escape. But Razumov, far from being the noble figure everyone imagines him to be, secretly betrays Haldin to the police. He does this to save his own skin, though he manages to convince himself that his real purpose is the good of Russia. The authorities, however, suspect Razumov himself of revolutionary sympathies. In order to remove their doubts, he allows himself to be persuaded by Mikulin, chief of czarist espionage, to become a secret agent for the government. He is sent to Geneva to spy on the Russian exiles plotting revolution there.

Ironically, the students and exiled revolutionaries continue to regard Razumov as a hero because, ignorant of what actually happened, they believe he did everything in his power to save Haldin. When Razumov arrives in Switzerland, the exiles greet him as a comrade, making his task of reporting on the activities of the czar's enemies ridiculously easy. He meets Haldin's sister Nathalie and falls in love with her. But the strain of his double life becomes more and more of a burden. His nerves begin to give way, and at last he develops a sense of moral outrage at himself for having betrayed Haldin to his death, for double-crossing the exiles, and for accepting Nathalie's love and admiration under false pretenses.

In the end the pressure of his divided self is too much to bear. He confesses everything, first to Nathalie, then to the revolutionists, and accepts their violent revenge almost with a sense of relief. In *The Secret Agent,* Verloc voluntarily chose the underground life and was perfectly at home in it. Razumov, by contrast, was forced into it against his will, because of circumstances beyond his control. He is another of those torn men whose ancestry can be traced back to Conrad's father.

Much of Razumov's story is seen through the eyes of an English professor of languages in Geneva who serves as narrator for part of the book. This prudent, sober, middle-aged man speaks Russian fluently and has become acquainted with the Russian exiles in Geneva. He too has met and secretly fallen in love with

Nathalie. Naturally, he is not enthusiastic about Razumov, and finds the Russians generally too violent, moody, and emotional for his taste.

Conrad uses the device of an English narrator in order to compare the West Europeans, and particularly the English, with the Slavs. The Westerners are certainly more democratic, tolerant, and "civilized" than the Russians, but the Russians live with an emotional intensity beyond the reach of the stodgy Swiss or the overdisciplined English. Conrad originally planned to call the novel *Razumov,* but changed the title to *Under Western Eyes,* thus emphasizing the contrast between East and West.

Conrad saw no difference between the autocratic, tyrannical czarist regime and the autocratic, tyrannical revolutionists who sought to overthrow it. Both sides expressed the barbaric soul of Russia. As individuals, attractive Russians do appear in the novel, but they are swept away by the destructive dynamism of the country.

When Garnett suggested that *Under Western Eyes* exposed Conrad's hatred of Russia, the author burst out indignantly:

There's as much or as little hatred in this book as in the Outcast of the Islands for instance. I don't expect you will believe me. You are so russianized that you don't know the truth when you see it—unless it smells of cabbage-soup when it at once secures your profound respect. But it is hard after lavishing "a wealth of tenderness" on Tekla and Sophia, to be charged with the rather low trick of putting one's hate into a novel. If you seriously think I have done that then my dear fellow let me tell you that you don't know what the accent of hate is.

Conrad's angry response—usually he was only too willing to accept Garnett's judgments—shows what a touchy subject it was for him. He could look at the Germans with contemptuous indifference, but the Russians churned up some deeply emotional part of himself which he could not so easily control.

Yet he claimed to be an impersonal observer of the Russian scene and vehemently rejected any charge of prejudice. His attitude, he insisted, was not the product of blind hatred, but rather was the honest conclusion of a detached observer. And he always cited *Under Western Eyes* as undeniable proof of his freedom from bias, of his ability to draw Russians as human beings rather than as monsters of evil.

The novel itself bears him out. True, some of the Russian characters in it illustrate Conrad's worst accusations against the Russian temperament. Ziemianitch is a drunken lout, General T— an uncompromising reactionary, Nikita a sadistic bully, and Peter Ivanovich a pompous egotist. But there are other Russian figures who are as humanly attractive as any characters in Conrad. Sophia Antonovna is generous and warmhearted. Mikulin is loyal and intelligent. Haldin is a high-minded idealist who refuses to give away his comrades even under torture. Tekla is devoted and self-sacrificing. Razumov does terrible things but suffers agonies of remorse which at last lead him to a kind of redemption. And in Nathalie Haldin, the heroine, Conrad created his most attractive young woman, as appealing in her youth as Mrs. Gould in her middle age.

Conrad the man was undoubtedly prejudiced; Conrad the artist was not. In the novel the distortions of the one were corrected by the commitment to psychological truth of the other. Art once again came to his aid, for he managed to control in the fiction of *Under Western Eyes* the powerful emotion that he could not master in his own life.

This novel about Russia was geographically as close as Conrad ever got in his major work to Poland. It was not close enough to suit various Poles. When Conrad left Poland as a youth, he was accused by relatives and friends of being a deserter, of abandoning his country when it needed him most. After he became a novelist in another language, Polish writers and intellectuals accused him of the same offense. He had put his talent at the service of another country and left Poland the poorer. How ungrateful it was of him, they said, to turn his back on the nation that had nurtured him. The bitterness of these remarks upset Conrad. They made him feel not so much guilty as unhappy. He was upset not because they were true but because they expressed so much bad feeling.

He did not share the sentiments of his accusers any more than he had accepted the charge of desertion at leaving Poland in the first place. On the personal plane, he kept up his Polish ties to the very end of his life. He corresponded in Polish with friends and relatives, returned to Poland several times to visit his uncle, supported the cause of Polish independence, and never stopped acknowledging his Polish origins. To him, these actions proved that he had never rejected Poland.

It is nevertheless true that he kept Poland out of his art, however closely related to Poland he remained in his life. His art, expressed in English, was his only hope of establishing some sort of English identity. Conrad did not want to be regarded as a Pole who had somehow strayed into the English language as an exotic outsider and who did not really belong there. He wanted very much to be taken for an English writer, since he obviously could never pass for an Englishman in his manner, appearance, or speech. The break with Poland had to be complete in his work, for there was no possibility of becoming completely English in any other form.

There was another, more immediately practical reason for the absence of Polish themes in his writing. In

the nineteenth century Poland was considered a remote backwater of Europe, of little interest to English
readers. Conrad sensed that stories on Polish subjects,
while highly appropriate in Poland, would be greeted
with indifference in England.

Malaya was another matter. England at that time had
Malay colonies, which would in itself guarantee public
attention. Rudyard Kipling had achieved an immense
success in England with his tales about India. Interest
in Empire themes was at its peak. Conrad had, indeed,
been hailed as a Kipling of the Far East with the appearance of *Almayer's Folly*. Moreover, his Malay
novels had Englishmen in them and were, in fact, dom-
inated by the presence of the Englishman Tom Lingard.

Russia was another country with a major attraction
for the English. She was crowding the British in the
Mediterranean and the Pacific. She was stirring up
trouble in India. England had fought the Crimean War
against her. Russia was regarded as a vast enigma still
to be revealed. *Under Western Eyes* had a timely and
fascinating subject for the English, an advantage to
which Conrad, anxious for popularity, was keenly
alert. No such advantage operated in the case of
Poland.

These considerations weighed heavily with Conrad
in the writing of his novels. There were many Poles, of
course, who did not see it that way, who saw only that
one of their gifted sons had deliberately turned his
back on Polish literature and chosen to enrich a for-

eign culture. Conrad was hurt by these accusations, but he did not accept them and did not believe them justified. In his own heart, he did not feel like a deserter. "All a man can betray is his conscience," Razumov exclaims in *Under Western Eyes*. With regard to Poland, Conrad's conscience was clear.

CHAPTER 17

Breakthrough

In November, 1909, while in the middle of *Under Western Eyes,* Conrad took time out to write "The Secret Sharer," one of his most powerful short stories. Like *Lord Jim* and other works, it was based on an actual incident at sea that Conrad had read about and then proceeded to change to suit his purposes, breathing into it the special atmosphere and moral energy that he himself once described as "Conradese."

The young captain in the story is about to assume his first command. The ship assigned to him is anchored in the Gulf of Siam. On the night before it is to sail, the captain is pacing the deck nervously, while the crew is asleep below. He is unsure of himself, wondering how, untested as he is, he will respond to the challenge ahead. He suddenly remembers that he has forgotten to haul up a rope ladder hanging over the ship's side. When he starts to pull it up, it feels unaccountably heavy and, looking down, he sees a naked man clinging to the bottom rung.

The captain helps the man aboard and discovers that he is Leggatt, first mate of the *Sephora,* anchored more than a mile away. Some weeks earlier, during a storm, Leggatt killed a panicking member of the crew while trying to subdue him. He was accused of murder and placed under arrest in his cabin. He waited for a chance to escape and, that night, managed to break out and jump overboard, determined to swim for his life. He felt he would rather risk drowning than be taken back to England and put on trial.

The captain is stirred by this tale of boldness and courage; he resolves to hide Leggatt in his cabin and help him escape during the voyage. He begins to think of Leggatt as being, in some mysterious way, his other self, his double. Leggatt is the man he would like to be. If the captain could discover in himself the resoluteness displayed by Leggatt, his doubts about his first command would be swept away. If the hunted man can be saved, then he, the captain, responsible for saving him, will have proved himself fit for any crisis. His experience with Leggatt becomes a kind of test or preview of his experience with the ship.

There now begins the nerve-racking ordeal of keeping Leggatt under cover. He must be hidden from the steward who comes to the cabin several times a day, and from the crew who already think their captain is behaving oddly. His presence must be concealed from the suspicious captain of the *Sephora* who comes aboard in search of the escaped prisoner.

After some days at sea, the captain, to the alarm of the puzzled crew, changes course and maneuvers the ship dangerously close to a rocky coastline in order to give Leggatt a chance to swim to safety. In so doing, he risks the vessel, the lives of the crew, his own life. But in succeeding, he proves his capacity and earns the right to his command. Leggatt swims away to his unknown destiny, and the captain sails off in his ship secure in the knowledge of his own discovered strength, the secret strength which, in setting Leggatt free, has by this very act released itself.

In Conrad's sea stories, the ship serves many functions. It is the link between man and nature: the sea makes itself felt and its movements known through the ship to the men on her. It is the arena in which men, common seamen and officers alike, meet those tests of courage and duty forced upon them by their remorseless and untiring friend-enemy, the sea. It challenges their skill, and skill is a Conradian ideal fully as important as courage, fidelity, and self-knowledge.

To do one's job not just routinely or even competently but supremely well is what lends grace and meaning to everyday tasks. Conrad despised not just the outright slacker like Donkin in *The Nigger of the 'Narcissus'* but also the man who scrapes by with only a minimum effort. The ship, by presenting to the men who run her a constant series of challenges to their

craftsmanship, is one of the great instruments for test-
ing skill and arousing pride in work. Since sailing ships
make greater demands on their crews than steamships
—run more and more by machines and less and less by
men—Conrad deplored the coming of the steam age as
a shrinking of human experience.

Ships are also mothers who shelter their children,
sweethearts who inspire adoration, beautiful objects
with trim lines and graceful movements which evoke
the joy and wonder that beauty stimulates in most
men. They are the agents that make voyages possible,
those magical voyages in Conrad which are journeys in
mind and spirit as well as in space, where men have
their encounters with danger, their collisions within the
floating society of shipboard, their brushes with death,
and where they discover their own hidden natures.

Yet he did not think of himself as a "sea" writer and
objected when other people did. His stories, he
claimed, were about men at sea rather than the sea itself, and he was forever saying that most of his books
took place on land, "that in the body of my work
barely one-tenth is what may be called sea stuff." He
grew very tired of the nautical label. "I do wish that all
those ships of mine were given a rest," he wrote plain-
tively a year before his death.

"The Secret Sharer" was the fifth of Conrad's sea
journeys. The earlier four were *The Nigger of the
'Narcissus,'* "Youth," "Typhoon," and "The End of the
Tether." The sixth and last was eventually to be *The
Shadow-Line.* "The Secret Sharer" appeared in 1912

as part of a volume of short stories called *'Twixt Land and Sea.* The other two stories in the collection were "A Smile of Fortune" and "Freya of the Seven Isles." Both deal with vampire women who fascinate and crush the men who come under their spell. Both seem in some way related to Conrad's own experience with Mlle. Rénouf, who had attracted him so strongly on the island of Mauritius more than twenty years before. "A Smile of Fortune" is of middling quality, but "Freya of the Seven Isles" is one of the most dreadfully bad stories Conrad ever wrote.

The publication of *Under Western Eyes* in 1911 did nothing to thaw the icy indifference of the reading public. Conrad took its failure with better grace than he had *Nostromo*'s. His hopes were fewer. He grumbled, of course, but did not explode into such outbursts of indignation and bitterness as had come from him earlier.

He had come to the end of his great trio of political novels, and was ready for a change of subject. As far back as 1905 he had been working intermittently on a novel called *Chance,* which he now took up in earnest. He spent most of 1911 and much of 1912 finishing it. The novel ran as a serial in the New York *Herald* for the first six months of 1912, and was published as a book in 1913.

In *Chance* Marlow appears again as narrator, for the fourth and last time. He is not quite the Marlow of "Heart of Darkness" and *Lord Jim,* probing deeply into himself and responding with sharp moral concern to the experiences of others. He has mellowed, softened, grown a little sentimental. With the help of other narrators, he describes the courtship and marriage of Flora and Captain Anthony, the principal event of *Chance,* without being personally involved.

The novel gives him an opportunity to deliver opinions on women, on financial tycoons like Flora's father, and on the decisive role of chance in human affairs. These subjects, while exercising his mind, do not touch his heart. He is far more the narrator, far less the emotional participant than before, and perhaps less interesting as a result. One cannot say that *Chance* is really about Marlow, as can be said of "Heart of Darkness." He is at the rim rather than at the center of the story.

At the center, almost for the first time in a novel by Conrad, is the theme of love. Flora's father is disgraced and jailed while she is still a girl. Farmed out to unsympathetic relatives and employers, she grows up convinced that she is unlovable. When Captain Anthony proposes to her, she believes he does so out of pity. He, on the other hand, thinks she accepts him not out of love but to be freed from loneliness and poverty. Both are of course wrong, but the misunderstandings get their marriage off to a bad start.

Their two closest relatives make things worse. Captain Anthony's sister, Mrs. Fyne, is a ferocious feminist who believes that women should dominate men and run the world. She dislikes Flora for not accepting her ideas; it is she who poisons her brother's mind about Flora's motives. Flora's father, the great financier de Barral, emerges from jail without a penny and hates his son-in-law, partly because he is dependent on him for food and lodging, partly because he wants his daughter all to himself.

After the wedding the three go off for a journey on Anthony's ship, the *Ferndale*. Days and weeks drift by while husband and wife remain painfully separated by their false ideas about each other. Captain Anthony, neglecting his duties as ship's master, spends hours staring dully at Flora while de Barral glowers angrily at him. The deadlock is finally broken when the financier attempts to murder his son-in-law. Quite by chance, de Barral is seen putting poison into Anthony's drink by young Powell, the second mate who is secretly in love with Flora himself. Powell stops Anthony from sipping the drink. In the ensuing hullabaloo, husband and wife recognize their real feelings for each other, and de Barral, in despair at being "abandoned" by his daughter, swallows the poison himself and dies.

Powell is one of the narrators of the novel; in the end he gets his reward by marrying Flora when, after some years, Captain Anthony conveniently drowns in an accident at sea. For this second marriage, Marlow serves as matchmaker, a tranquil conclusion to the many roles he has played in Conrad's fiction.

Chance is not to be ranked with Conrad's major works, but it is an absorbing psychological study. The principal characters are boldly drawn, with the hero and heroine eventually revealed as the reverse of what

they at first appear to be. Captain Anthony is competent and controlled on the surface; inwardly he is
mushy and soft. Flora appears helpless and pathetic on
the surface; inside, she is highly competent and even
aggressive. Mrs. Fyne is a man-eating feminist. De
Barral is so wrapped up in himself that he is utterly
blind to others. Flora's governess, like all of Conrad's
villains, like Donkin in *The Nigger,* Massy in "The
End of the Tether," and Sotillo in *Nostromo,* flies into
rages out of all proportion to the cause. Everyone in
the novel tilts dangerously toward one emotional abyss
or another. Everyone except Marlow, and he is not
really involved.

Chance is a bit short on depth and substance. Its
narrative machinery is too large for the story. But it
was the novel that won Conrad his first public success.
In England it sold four times as many copies as *Under
Western Eyes;* in America the ratio was even higher.
Helped by its serialization in a prominent New York
newspaper, the book sold so briskly that it transformed
Conrad overnight from a marginal writer to a best
seller.

In England the change was not that spectacular, yet
it was real enough. Conrad never became a really
wealthy man, but the success of *Chance* and the books
that followed enabled him to pay off his debt to Pinker.
He was able to plan extended vacations outside of England, and eventually to move into the comfortable
house near Canterbury where the Conrads lived during his last years. Most of all, the grinding pressure of
money at last began to lift, though he had become so

used to it that he did not feel the relief as keenly as he would have ten years earlier. *"Chance* had a tremendous press," he wrote. "How I would have felt about it ten or eight years ago I can't say. Now I can't even pretend I am elated. If I had *Nostromo, The Nigger, Lord Jim,* in my desk or only in my head, I would feel differently no doubt."

What was there about *Chance* that caught the public fancy? Perhaps the fact that it was a love story, and the general reader is always hungry for romance. Big business scandals are always in the news; the one involving de Barral is handled very dramatically. An event of great topical interest in 1912 and 1913 was the feminist movement, with suffragettes clamoring for the vote and chaining themselves to the railings of Parliament to protest the inferior position of women. Mrs. Fyne is a powerful reflection of the movement and must have seemed to the readers of the day to be drawn straight from life. The story is filled with other familiar characters: the appealing heroine, the gallant gentlemanly hero, the dominating and possessive father—these were standard figures in popular fiction. Dressing them up, as Conrad did, in the latest turns of modern psychological theory only added to their appeal. Or perhaps the success of *Chance* was largely a matter of chance.

The reading public is notoriously fickle. Having ignored Conrad for eighteen years, it now mysteriously reversed itself and took him to its heart. It continued to do so to the end of his life. Having endured eighteen years of adversity as a writer, Conrad now enjoyed twelve final years of prosperity. At first, not one of his books had succeeded. From *Chance* on, not one of his books failed.

The reading public was fickle not only in its timing but also in its taste. Conrad's great period as a writer ended almost at the point when he began being popular. *Chance* is a far cry from *Under Western Eyes,* and the later novels, *The Arrow of Gold, The Rescue, The Rover,* are not to be compared with *Lord Jim* and *Nostromo* or even with *Almayer's Folly.* The decline in his art is in nearly exact proportion to the rise in his popular success. Only two works of this last period reveal the earlier excellence. One, the short novel *The Shadow-Line,* belongs with his supreme accomplishments. The other, *Victory,* is marred by a good deal of shoddy and uneven writing, yet the portrait of its fascinating principal figure, Axel Heyst, redeems its shortcomings.

But the merit of the individual work did not seem to matter. Once the breakthrough came with *Chance,* readers in large and increasing numbers bought every Conrad book in sight. The long public freeze was now followed by a brisk public boom. No one was more surprised than Conrad. He had trained himself not to expect it. Yet the fact that it came with the wrong books and years after it would have done him the most good did not prevent him from accepting and enjoying it.

Having already granted Conrad the satisfactions of achievement, literature now belatedly rewarded him with financial success.

CHAPTER 18

War

It was, of course, only coincidence that Conrad called his next novel *Victory*. The title nonetheless reflected his changed condition. The unexpected popularity of *Chance* had lifted him out of obscurity and hardship and made him a success in the eyes of the world. This was a victory indeed. Conrad felt the effects of this victory in the eased circumstances of his life, though he did not acknowledge them openly as, earlier, he had dwelt on the bitterness of failure.

Axel Heyst, the hero of *Victory,* is the last of a long line of men in Conrad's work who live in isolation. Almayer was isolated by his inflamed vanity, Jim by his inflated dream of heroism, Decoud by his skeptical intelligence, Razumov by his lack of personal ties. Heyst's father, a gloomy philosopher, had brought up his son to distrust human nature and avoid connections. At the start of the book, the forty-year-old Heyst is sitting on the porch of his house on an abandoned island in the Dutch East Indies. The burning ash at the end of his cheroot is seen against the smoke rising from the crater of a nearby sleeping volcano. Except for a Chinese servant, he is absolutely alone.

Heyst's carefully created solitude does not last long. His natural sympathy for people in trouble leads him to rescue and carry off to his island a girl who was being abused by her employers and by the hotel keeper Schomberg. The same element in his nature moves him also to intervene in the business affairs of a trader about to go bankrupt. These events set into motion all kinds of slanderous rumors and gossip about his motives. The gossip is stirred up chiefly by the envious Schomberg and leads to misunderstandings which prove fatal.

Three grotesquely villainous cutthroats appear at Schomberg's hotel. To get rid of them, Schomberg sends them off to Heyst's island after treasure which, according to rumor, Heyst is supposed to have buried. A series of sensational events now occur: assaults, fires, ambuscades, last-minute rescues, murders, and suicide. In the end the girl sacrifices herself to save Heyst in the hope of proving to him that she really loves him. Heyst wants to love her, but he has lived alone so long that he has forgotten how to release his feelings. The villains are finally defeated, but the girl's death leads Heyst, in despair at his own inability to live as a warmhearted human being, to kill himself. The novel concludes with Heyst's realization, expressed in his last words, that men must learn "while young to hope, to love—and to . . . trust in life!"

Victory bogs down at times in overblown writing and melodrama. The girl Lena is too simply drawn for the role she is asked to play, and the three villains are outrageous caricatures. The novel is held together by Schomberg and Heyst, both superbly drawn figures. Placed at opposite poles of the action, they represent the contrasting principles of human nature: Schomberg, all cunning and meddlesome interference; Heyst, all aristocratic and fastidious withdrawal. Between them they make *Victory* a greater achievement than *Chance,* though even they are not powerful enough to transform it into absolutely first-class Conrad.

Victory was a great financial success. Pinker got Conrad a handsome advance for it. With the money, Conrad paid off what remained of the debt to his agent and made preparations for a trip to Poland. The novel was finished in June, 1914, and in July the Conrads set out for Eastern Europe. More than twenty years had passed since Conrad had last visited his native land. He was eager to have his sons see Poland. What Mrs. Conrad called his "homing instinct" had become stronger as the years advanced.

They crossed the North Sea, traveled through Germany, and reached Cracow late in July. The sight of the city where he had spent his schooldays filled Conrad with an intense and nostalgic pleasure. Jessie was stirred by his feelings, as she was by her first visit to his native country. Yet she could not help commenting on how badly the streets were paved and wrinkling her nose at the smell from the drains, whereupon Conrad turned upon her indignantly to remind her that they were not in England.

They had barely arrived when Russian troops on one side of Poland and an army of the Austro-Hungarian Empire on another began mobilizing. On the first of August World War I broke out.

The agitation and confusion inside Poland were tremendous. Conrad felt it advisable to get away from Cracow, now rapidly turning into an Austrian garrison town, to some quieter place. The Conrads thereupon moved to Zankopane, a hundred kilometers away. Conrad wanted to remain in Poland as long as he could, but as the prospect of England declaring war on Austria grew greater he realized the danger to himself as a possible enemy alien. He decided to leave.

This was no longer easy. The trains were being commandeered to transport troops, and all ordinary civilian schedules were cancelled. Uncertainty mounted from day to day, aggravated by the final declarations of war between the Allies and the Central Powers. To add to the confusion, England and Russia were now fighting on the same side, arousing in Conrad an intense division of loyalties. He wanted England to win, of course, but if this meant Russia winning too, that would make Poland's cause more hopeless than ever.

What with political complications and personal danger, it was a feverish time. Yet he seemed to thrive on the excitement. "My health is good," he wrote to Pinker. "I am getting a mental stimulus out of this affair—I can tell you! And if it were not for the unavoidable anxiety I would derive much benefit from the experience."

In August he wrote a series of letters to England asking for money, but they were all returned. The war had interrupted postal service. By the middle of September the situation had become much worse. Conrad's cash was almost gone; the Conrads were without warm clothing, and Jessie's injured knee was troubling her again. The only news they received about the war was from German sources, and it was all bad. There were stories that the British fleet had been sunk and whole British armies destroyed. England herself was endlessly jeered at as despicable and inhumane. This barrage of propaganda further depressed Jessie's spirits and aggravated Conrad's growing alarm. To Borys and John, however, the whole experience was a thrilling adventure.

Conrad, deeply worried, was once more moving heaven and earth trying to get out of Poland. He was even more anxious to do so than he had been forty years earlier when he had left Poland for the first time. The circumstances were vastly different, but now as then departure proved difficult.

Not until October 7 were the Conrads at last able to leave Zankopane. They managed to hire an open carriage, and in a snowstorm drove thirty miles to the nearest railway station. There, they eventually got on

an army train for Cracow, the train "smelling of disin-
fectants and resounding with groans." It took eighteen
hours to cover the fifty miles to the old university city.
In Cracow they spent more wearying hours waiting for
a train to Vienna that had space for them to squeeze
into. Jessie remembered the wounded soldiers who
kept arriving from the front, the blood dripping to the
floor as they were carried through the station. When
they finally got aboard a train, the trip dragged along
for twenty-six hours on a journey that ordinarily took
five.

In Vienna Conrad collapsed from exhaustion and
spent five days in bed. Through the help of the American ambassador to Austria, Frederick Penfield, the
Conrads received a military pass from the Austrian
government allowing them to travel through Austrian
territory. With this pass, they at last reached the Italian
frontier and crossed over to safety late in October.
Two weeks later the Austrians, unaware that the Conrads had already left the country, rescinded the pass
and issued an order forbidding them to leave. By this
time the Conrads were already on a Dutch boat on the
way back to England, spared by a narrow margin the
grim experience of having to spend four years in an
Austrian internment camp.

They reached England on November 3, and Conrad
at once retired to bed with a severe attack of the gout.
In the days that followed, he had time to reflect on the
hardships and excitements of his journey to Poland,
the last he was ever to make, and on the tragedy that

was engulfing Europe. He was conscious of what he owed to Penfield, a debt that he was to discharge as only a writer could. He dedicated one of his later novels, *The Rescue,* to the American diplomat who had saved him and his family from untold difficulties.

The bleak war years now set in. Conrad was worried over the fate of his friends and relatives in war-torn Poland. He felt that private life and even literature were somehow trivial when Europe was in such upheaval and tens of thousands of men were being slaughtered. Borys Conrad came of military age in 1916 and joined an artillery unit in France. He saw extensive action at the front until almost the very end of the war. This was a source of perpetual agony to his parents. Conrad used to give way to fantasies in which he shudderingly imagined that his son was dead. Nine hundred thousand British soldiers were killed in the First World War, virtually a whole generation wiped out in four brief years. Borys was one of the fortunate; though hospitalized by poison gas, he survived.

Conrad did little writing during this anguished period. One of the stories he did write, *The Shadow-Line* in 1915, was dedicated to Borys and to the whole generation of young men undergoing their supreme trial. The young merchant marine officer in the story undergoes a supreme trial too, a trial of nerves and life emptiness rather than war; he finally succeeds in crossing the shadow-line from youth to early maturity. *The Shadow-Line* was originally called *First Command,* and is another of those tales, like "The Secret Sharer," where a crisis of the mind is tied up with the command of a ship.

In 1888 Conrad had suddenly quit his post on the *Vidar*. He had then hung about restlessly on shore, and was about to return to Europe when he was unexpectedly offered his first command, the captaincy of the *Otago*. More or less the same thing happens to the protagonist of *The Shadow-Line*. Two crises occur in the story, with one an introduction to the other. In the first the sailor leaves his ship for no visible reason. He is fed up, not just with his job but with everything, fed up with living itself. Life has lost its savor for no reason in particular. Irritable and depressed, not knowing what to do with himself next, he stays for a time in the Officers' Home at Singapore. There, matters get worse. The other guests depress him still further. He considers them snobs and bores, and gradually sinks into deeper and deeper gloom. Just at the point when he is about to crack up altogether, he is invited to take command of a ship in Bangkok whose captain has died at sea.

This sudden change in fortune acts as a tonic to his shattered spirits. His interest in the world around him revives. He travels eagerly to Bangkok and assumes his first command with enthusiasm. The first crisis is over. The second is about to begin. It is the crisis of the ship. No sooner does it put into the Gulf of Siam than the crew comes down with cholera. The first mate is ill to start with. Only our captain and Ransome, the cook, an able man with a weak heart, remain healthy. As a final disaster, the wind disappears, forcing the vessel to drift helplessly in the Gulf while the men groan with fever and the captain discovers to his horror that the quinine bottles are empty. The ship's doldrums are exactly like the captain's doldrums in the first crisis. The two disasters are the same.

The dark night of the captain's soul is paralleled by the dark night of illness and inertia through which the ship passes. The captain despairs, but the fact that he has gone through his own ordeal, plus the cheerful courage of Ransome and of the uncomplaining crew, enables him to hang on. At last the wind springs up, the ship moves, the wholesome air of the open sea dissipates the last of the plague. Captain and ship have earned their right to each other by sharing and surviving a common trial. The captain crosses the shadow-line for a second time, leaving the doldrums behind. By saving the ship, he has won his way back to the society of men. He is no longer a "loner" living solely within himself, but a man securely anchored in the world.

With *The Shadow-Line,* Conrad rose to his last superb climax as a writer. Three more novels and part of a fourth still lay ahead, but these were the products of an increasingly weary man whose great work was behind him. The war added considerably to the exhaustion of his nervous energies. Worrying about the state of Europe and the safety of his son was a constant drain on his spirit. His writing fell off in vitality.

In 1916 he wrote two minor stories, "A Warrior's Soul" and "The Tale," both dealing with men at war. In

1917, at the government's invitation, he spent two weeks on a navy patrol boat in the North Sea, a return to his old element that he found stimulating. In that year also he began writing the prefaces, or Author's Notes as they came to be called, for a proposed collected edition of his works, and made a start on his next novel, *The Arrow of Gold*. This was completed in the summer of 1918. Conrad had few illusions about its quality even before he came to the end. "No colour, no relief, no tonality; the thinnest possible squeaky bubble," was how he described *The Arrow of Gold*. "And when I've finished with it, I shall go out and sell it in a market place for 20 times the money I had for the *Nigger,* 30 times the money I had for the *Mirror of the Sea.*"

Conrad was right about the money which his new work was bringing. This was the popular success he had always longed for. Now, however, it meant much less to him than it would have in the struggling early years.

His gout had grown much worse. His hands and fingers were so stiffened that much of *The Arrow of Gold* had to be dictated. In the novel Conrad goes back to the events of his youth in Marseilles, with the young hero running guns for the Carlists and falling in love with Doña Rita. He also fights a duel in which he is gravely wounded, the fictitious duel believed for so long to be autobiographically true. As an exercise in memory, *The Arrow of Gold* is an unreliable guide to Conrad's early life. As a work of art, it ranks near the bottom if not at the bottom of the novels. The narrative is curiously rigid: the characters assume fixed positions; the incidents do not flow into one another but are static in the manner of still photographs; the story tends to freeze rather than move.

Shortly after *The Arrow of Gold* was completed, the war came to an end. A year before, in 1917, the Bolshevik Revolution had broken out, and Russia soon withdrew from the Allied side and then from the war altogether. Conrad regarded this as still another sign of Russia's treachery and unreliability, and gloomily greeted the event as something he had expected. But with the final defeat of Germany, an event took place that did surprise him and filled him with joy. Poland was liberated and her independence proclaimed. Conrad had been convinced that this would not occur in the foreseeable future, at the very least not in his lifetime. It took a world war to accomplish it, but now, after a century and a half of partition, Poland was at last restored to herself.

As a civilized European, Conrad was deeply relieved by the end of the war. As a father, he was profoundly grateful that his son was spared. As a Pole, he rejoiced in the freedom of his native country, all the more because it was unexpected. These several emotions made 1918 and 1919 gratifying years to him, both personally and historically.

CHAPTER 19

"Sleep after Toyle"

After the war Conrad struggled against increasing weariness. "I have had in one way or another," he wrote to Galsworthy in 1922, "a pretty bad time. The reaction from the war, anxiety about Jessie, the growing sense of my own deficiencies have combined to make anything but a bed of roses for my aging bones. My very soul is aching all over." The "anxiety about Jessie" involved her injured leg, which required several new and expensive operations. Aside from concern over her health, Conrad was worried about the medical bills. These were so large that they made serious inroads even in the substantial income he was enjoying from the success of his books.

Conrad's last novels reflect his flagging energy. *The Rescue* (1920) deals with an episode early in Tom Lingard's life. This was the novel Conrad had started back in the 1890s and then, after some years of frustrating effort, given up. The unfinished manuscript had remained in a drawer since the beginning of the century. He took it out again late in 1918, found the romantic theme in the book easier to work with, overhauled the finished chapters, and went on to complete the story.

In *The Rescue* Lingard, the busybody who loves to arrange and improve other people's lives, dedicates himself to restoring a noble young Malay prince named Hassan to his throne. At a crucial moment a yacht manned by Europeans on a pleasure cruise runs aground. Lingard is forced to choose between the interests of the Malays and the safety of the whites, a choice he finds himself unable to make. Up till this point he has been vigorous and decisive. Now he abruptly sinks into a dreamlike immobility.

He falls in love with Mrs. Travers, the discontented wife of the yacht owner. This undermines him altogether, and he becomes totally incapable of action. He allows events to drift until all his elaborately prepared plans for Hassan are completely ruined. The yacht is refloated and leaves with Mrs. Travers still aboard. Lingard loses out in both politics and love. He is left more dazed than ever, a man very different from the masterful and aggressive figure of Conrad's first two Malayan novels and the opening of this one.

The plot of *The Rescue* is very intricate, but the characters are not. Their feelings are vague, their motives obscure. The reasons for Lingard's sudden lapse into a trancelike state are never really convincing. Conrad is still able to describe outer shapes and movements, but getting at the inner selves of his men and women now seems beyond his grasp. These later novels all have well-constructed frames, but the interiors are lacking.

His last completed novel was *The Rover*. The principal figure is Jean Peyrol, a very old seaman and ex-pirate who has retired to a farm near Toulon to live out his remaining years in rural serenity. But the times are against him. Napoleon is at war with England, and Nelson's fleet is hovering offshore.

Left to his own devices, Peyrol would be content to doze in the sun. But a pair of young lovers in whom he takes an interest draw him out of his retirement. The young man, a French naval lieutenant, is on a dangerous assignment to lure Nelson away with faked dispatches. He must pretend to run the British blockade, and permit himself to be overtaken and captured so that the false dispatches can be found on him. If he is killed in the pursuit, so much the better, for this will convince the British that the papers are authentic.

Peyrol resolves to take the lieutenant's place. He is old, after all, and has nothing to lose. He tricks the younger man and takes off on his patriotic mission in his stead. Pursued by an English frigate, Peyrol does not yield but fires at his pursuers and with great skill "tries" to get away. The English fire back. Peyrol is killed. The papers are found on his body as planned. Nelson sails off on the false trail, and the French win the day.

Peyrol's situation is close to Conrad's heart. The seaman is old. He returns to his native land after a lifetime's absence. He sacrifices his life for his country from personal rather than political motives. The novel moves at a slow, dignified pace in keeping with the advanced years of its aged hero. But for long stretches nothing happens, and Peyrol himself is too hollow a figure to fill the vacuum. There are beautiful descriptions of the Mediterranean and, toward the end, a brief burst of exciting action. These are scarcely enough to keep the book from being anything more than a graceful elegy to an aging man.

The year in which *The Rover* was written, 1922, also witnessed the appearance of James Joyce's novel *Ulysses* and T. S. Eliot's poem *The Waste Land*. These were the masterpieces of the generation following Conrad. Joyce was twenty-five years younger than Conrad; Eliot, thirty. Like him, both were exiles from their own countries.

Only one more work of fiction remained, the unfinished novel *Suspense*. This too had a Napoleonic background. Conrad did a good deal of reading for it at the British Museum, and in 1921 took a vacation in Corsica during which he gathered firsthand impressions. The novel went slowly. At the same time he was collecting his scattered essays for publication and turning *The Secret Agent* into a play. It was performed briefly in 1922 but was not a success.

In 1923 he visited the United States, staying as house guest for some weeks in the Long Island home of his American publisher. There he gave a public reading of scenes from *Victory,* the only such reading of his career. The occasion went off well, but Conrad was too self-conscious about his accent and generally too tense to repeat it. The public platform, on which writers like Dickens had sparkled, was not Conrad's natural medium.

In his last years Conrad enjoyed the benefits of his growing fame. The first collected edition of his works came out in 1920, a kind of immortality for a still-living author. His books were translated into French, German, and Polish. He had achieved a great success with both critics and the general public.

People from all over the world, some of them aspiring writers, came to visit him. He received a great many letters asking about the meaning of his books, requesting advice and guidance, or presenting literary questions. He sat for a bust by the distinguished sculptor Jacob Epstein, and was offered a knighthood by the British government. Friends and disciples like Jean-Aubry and Richard Curle took down his conversations, gathered facts about his life in preparation for biographies, and surrounded him with admiration. He had become a celebrity. Final proof of his new status was supplied in 1923 by the highly publicized auction in New York of the John Quinn library. The Conrad manuscripts bought by Quinn over the years for modest sums were sold to dealers and collectors at record prices.

But Conrad was growing conscious of advancing age. Early in 1922 his agent, J. B. Pinker, died. Conrad was deeply affected. "I need not tell you how profoundly I feel the loss of J. B. Pinker," he wrote to his publisher in America, "my friend of twenty years' standing, whose devotion to my interests and whose affection borne towards myself and all belonging to me were the greatest moral and material support through nearly all my writing life." Other men he had known were dying too. The sense of mortality, always acute in Conrad, was now stronger than ever.

In the summer of 1924 Conrad was carrying on with his usual routine, working intermittently on *Suspense,* answering letters, refusing invitations from magazine editors to contribute articles, taking care of Jessie when she was laid up in bed, and nursing his own ailments. On August 2 he spent most of the day working at his desk. Then at eight-thirty the next morning, with no warning at all, he suffered a sudden heart attack and died within minutes. He was sixty-six.

Four days later he was buried at Canterbury. The funeral was attended by his wife, sons, and close friends of long standing including Garnett, Cunningham Grahame, Jean-Aubry, and Curle. A personal representative of the Polish Minister to England was also present. On the tombstone appeared the lines from

Spenser that had been printed on the title page of *The Rover:*

Sleep after toyle, port after stormie seas,
Ease after warre, death after life, does greatly
please.

At the end of his life Conrad was an honored and eminent man, a position he had earned through his own heroic exertions. He had had two careers and achieved a mastery of each. As a seaman he had lived almost wholly in the physical sphere; as a writer, almost wholly in the mind. He embraced the two sides of human existence.

Conrad was one of the great modern novelists. He explored profoundly the moral landscape of the mind, finding there the subtle flaws as well as hidden strengths that govern and complicate human behavior. He transformed geography into a great dramatic spectacle and infused the physical world with a richness of psychological meaning that prepared the way for the work of Proust and Joyce. His influence extended to the generation of younger writers that came later, to O'Neill, Fitzgerald, Hemingway, and Faulkner.

For these achievements, Conrad's name will endure in literature. In a more personal sense, however, his life is an example of pressures and difficulties overcome, and courage displayed. It stands as one of the remarkable human records of the age.

A SELECTED
BIBLIOGRAPHY

By Conrad

(Dates represent first publication in book form)

FICTION

1895   *Almayer's Folly*

1896   *An Outcast of the Islands*

1898   *The Nigger of the 'Narcissus'*

1898   *Tales of Unrest* ("Karain," "The Idiots," "An Outpost of Progress," "The Lagoon," "The Return")

1900   *Lord Jim*

1901   *The Inheritors* (with Ford Madox Hueffer)

1902   *Youth, and Two Other Stories* ("Youth," "Heart of Darkness," "The End of the Tether")

1903   *Typhoon, and Other Stories* ("Typhoon," "Falk," "Amy Foster," "Tomorrow")

1903   *Romance* (with Ford Madox Hueffer)

1904   *Nostromo*

198

1907 *The Secret Agent*
1908 *A Set of Six* ("Gaspar Ruiz," "The Informer," "The Brute," "An Anarchist," "The Duel," "Il Conde")
1911 *Under Western Eyes*
1912 *'Twixt Land and Sea* ("A Smile of Fortune," "The Secret Sharer," "Freya of the Seven Isles")
1913 *Chance*
1915 *Victory*
1915 *Within the Tides* ("The Planter of Malata," "The Partner," "The Inn of the Two Witches," "Because of the Dollars")
1917 *The Shadow-Line*
1919 *The Arrow of Gold*
1920 *The Rescue*
1923 *The Rover*
1924 *The Nature of a Crime* (with Ford Madox Hueffer)
1925 *Suspense*
1925 *Tales of Hearsay* ("The Warrior's Soul," "Prince Roman," "The Tale," "The Black Mate")
1928 *The Sisters*

DRAMA

1917 *One Day More* (adaptation of "Tomorrow")
1921 *The Secret Agent* (adaptation of the novel)
1923 *Laughing Anne* (adaptation of "Because of the Dollars")

NONFICTION

1906 *The Mirror of the Sea*
1912 *A Personal Record*
1921 *Notes on Life and Letters*
1926 *Last Essays*
1937 *Conrad's Prefaces to His Works,* introd. Edward Garnett

The most comprehensive recent edition of Conrad's writings is *The Collected Edition of the Works of Joseph Conrad*. 21 vols. London: J. M. Dent, 1946–1955. The following are the principal collections of Conrad's letters to appear in English:

Joseph Conrad's Letters to His Wife, pref. Jessie Conrad. London: Privately printed by *The Bookman's Journal,* 1927.

Jean-Aubry, G. *Joseph Conrad: Life and Letters.* 2 vols. Garden City, N.Y.: Doubleday, Doran, 1927.

Conrad to a Friend, 150 Selected Letters from Joseph Conrad to Richard Curle, ed. with introd. and notes by Richard Curle. New York: Crosby Gaige, 1928.

Letters from Joseph Conrad, 1895–1924, ed. with introd. by Edward Garnett. Indianapolis: Bobbs-Merrill, 1928.

Letters of Joseph Conrad to Marguerite Poradowska, 1890–1920, tr. and ed. John A. Gee and Paul J. Sturm. New Haven: Yale University Press, 1940.

Letters of Joseph Conrad to William Blackwood and David S. Meldrum, ed. William Blackburn. Durham, N.C.: Duke University Press, 1958.

Conrad's Polish Background: Letters to and from Polish Friends, ed. Zdzislaw Najder, tr. Halina Carroll. New York: Oxford University Press, 1964.

About Conrad

BAINES, JOCELYN. *Joseph Conrad: A Critical Biography.* New York: McGraw-Hill, 1960.

CONRAD, JESSIE. *Joseph Conrad and His Circle.* New York: Dutton, 1935.

———. *Joseph Conrad As I Knew Him.* New York: Doubleday, Page, 1926.

FORD, FORD MADOX. *Joseph Conrad, A Personal Remembrance*. Boston: Little, Brown, 1924.

GORDAN, JOHN DOZIER. *Joseph Conrad: The Making of a Novelist*. Cambridge, Mass.: Harvard University Press, 1940.

GUÉRARD, ALBERT J. *Conrad the Novelist*. Cambridge, Mass.: Harvard University Press, 1958.

GURKO, LEO. *Joseph Conrad: Giant in Exile*. New York: Macmillan, 1962.

HAY, ELOISE KNAPP. *The Political Novels of Joseph Conrad*. Chicago: University of Chicago Press, 1963.

HEWITT, DOUGLAS. *Conrad: A Reassessment*. Cambridge, Eng.: Bowes and Bowes, 1952.

JEAN-AUBRY, G. *The Sea Dreamer: A Definitive Biography of Joseph Conrad*, tr. Helen Sebba. Garden City, N.Y.: Doubleday, 1957.

KEATING, GEORGE T. *A Conrad Memorial Library*. Garden City, N.Y.: Doubleday, Doran, 1929.

KIMBROUGH, ROBERT, ed. *Heart of Darkness*. Text, sources, essays in criticism. New York: Norton, 1963.

LEAVIS, F. R. *The Great Tradition*. London: Chatto and Windus, 1948.

LOHF, KENNETH A., AND EUGENE P. SHEEHY. *Joseph Conrad at Mid-Century: Editions and Studies, 1895–1955*. Minneapolis: University of Minnesota Press, 1957.

MILOSZ, CZESLAW. "Joseph Conrad in Polish Eyes." *The Atlantic Monthly* (November, 1957).

Modern Fiction Studies (Fall, 1955, and Spring, 1964). Two special numbers devoted to Conrad, each containing a checklist of criticism on his work.

MORF, GUSTAV. *The Polish Heritage of Joseph Conrad*. London: Sampson Low, Marston, 1930.

MOSER, THOMAS. *Joseph Conrad: Achievement and Decline*. Cambridge, Mass.: Harvard University Press, 1957.

STALLMAN, R. W., ed. *A Critical Symposium on Joseph Conrad.* East Lansing, Mich.: Michigan State University Press, 1960.

VAN GHENT, DOROTHY. *The English Novel: Form and Function.* New York: Rinehart, 1953.

WARREN, ROBERT PENN. Introduction to *Nostromo.* New York: Modern Library, 1951.

WATT, IAN. "Story and Idea in Conrad's *The Shadow-Line." The Critical Quarterly* (Summer, 1960).

YOUNG, VERNON. "Trial by Water: Joseph Conrad's *The Nigger of the 'Narcissus.'" Accent* (Spring, 1952).

ZABEL, MORTON DAUWEN. "Joseph Conrad: Chance and Recognition." *Sewanee Review* (Winter, 1945).

INDEX

ABOUT THE AUTHOR

Leo Gurko is professor of English at Hunter College in New York and served as chairman of the department from 1954 to 1960. Educated at the College of the City of Detroit and the University of Wisconsin, he is the author of *The Angry Decade; Heroes, Highbrows and the Popular Mind; Tom Paine, Freedom's Apostle;* and *Joseph Conrad: Giant in Exile.*

At various times Dr. Gurko has worked as an advertising copy writer, translator, free-lance editor, and publisher's reader. He has made frequent appearances on radio and television, and has written many articles on modern English and American literature.

A year in Europe with his family in 1953–1954 was made possible by a grant from the Ford Foundation. In 1958–1959 he spent a second year in Europe, this time on sabbatical leave.

Among his avocations are tennis, travel, the operas of Mozart and Verdi, and professional baseball. He and his wife, herself an author of biographies for younger readers, live in New York City. They have a son and daughter.